THE BROTHERS KARAMAZOV

Borgo Press Drama Translations by FRANK J. MORLOCK

Alcestis, by Philippe Quinault * *Anna Karenina*, by Edmond Guiraud, from Leo Tolstoy * *Anthony*, by Alexandre Dumas * *Atys*, by Philippe Quinault * *The Boss Lady*, by Paul Féval * *The Brothers Karamazov*, by Jacques Copeau & Jean Croué * *The Children of Captain Grant*, by Jules Verne & Adolphe d'Ennery * *Cleopatra*, by Victorien Sardou * *Crime and Punishment*, by Frank J. Morlock, from Fyodor Dostoyevsky * *Don Quixote*, by Victorien Sardou, from Miguel de Cervantes * *The Dream of a Summer Night*, by Paul Meurice * *Falstaff*, by William Shakespeare, John Dennis, William Kendrick, & Frank J. Morlock * *The Idiot*, by Frank J. Morlock, from Fyodor Dostoyevsky * *Isis*, by Philippe Quinault * *Jesus of Nazareth*, by Paul Demasy * *The Jew of Venice*, by Ferdinand Dugué * *Joan of Arc*, by Charles Desnoyer * *The Lily of the Valley*, by Théodore Barrière & Arthur de Beauplan, from Honoré de Balzac * *Lord Byron in Venice*, by Jacques Ancelot * *Louis XIV and the Affair of the Poisons*, by Victorien Sardou * *The Man Who Saw the Devil*, by Gaston Leroux * *The Marriage of Hamlet*, by Jean Sarment * *Mathias Sandorf*, by Jules Verne & William Busnach * *Michael Strogoff*, by Jules Verne & Adolphe d'Ennery * *Les Misérables*, by Victor Hugo, Paul Meurice, & Charles Victor Hugo * *Monte Cristo, Parts One* through *Four*, by Alexandre Dumas * *The Musketeers*, by Alexandre Dumas * *The Mysteries of Paris*, by Eugène Sue & Prosper Dinaux * *Napoléon Bonaparte*, by Alexandre Dumas * *Ninety-Three*, by Victor Hugo & Paul Meurice * *Notes from the Underground*, by Frank J. Morlock, from Fyodor Dostoyevsky * *Outrageous Women: Lady MacBeth and Other French Plays*, edited by Frank J. Morlock * *Peau de Chagrin*, by Louis Judicis, from Honoré de Balzac * *The Prisoner of the Bastille*, by Alexandre Dumas * *A Raw Youth*, by Frank J. Morlock, from Fyodor Dostoyevsky * *Richard Darlington*, by Alexandre Dumas * *The San Felice*, by Maurice Drack, from Alexandre Dumas * *Saul and David*, by Voltaire * *Shylock, the Merchant of Venice*, by Alfred de Vigny * *Socrates*, by Voltaire * *The Son of Porthos*, by Émile Blavet, from M. Paul Mahalin * *The Stendhal Hamlet Scenarios and Other Shakespearean Shorts from the French*, edited by Frank J. Morlock * *A Summer Night's Dream*, by Joseph-Bernard Rosier & Adolphe de Leuwen * *The Three Musketeers*, by Alexandre Dumas * *Urbain Grandier and the Devils of Loudon*, by Alexandre Dumas * *The Voyage Through the Impossible*, by Jules Verne & Adolphe d'Ennery * *War and Peace*, by J. Wladimir Bienstock & Charles Martel * *The Whites and the Blues*, by Alexandre Dumas * *William Shakespeare*, by Ferdinand Dugué

THE BROTHERS KARAMAZOV

A PLAY IN FIVE ACTS

JACQUES COPEAU &

JEAN CROUÉ

Edited and Translated by Frank J. Morlock
Adapted from the Novel by Fyodor Dostoyevsky

THE BORGO PRESS
MMXI

THE BROTHERS KARAMAZOV

Copyright © 2011 by Frank J. Morlock

FIRST EDITION

Published by Wildside Press LLC

www.wildsidebooks.com

DEDICATION

For My Friends,

Doris Bergmann and Richard McDonald

CONTENTS

Cast of Characters 9
Act I 11
Act II 55
Act III. 89
Act IV. 127
Act V 157
About the Editor 197

CAST OF CHARACTERS

Feodor Pavlovitch Karamazov
Ivan Feodorovitch Karamazov
Dimitri Feodorovitch Karamazov
Alexei (Alyosha) Feodorovitch Karamazov
Smerdiakov
Father Zossima
Gregori Vassiliev
Moussialovitch
Vroubelski
Trifon Boristch
Coachman Andre
Chief of Police
Father Paissi
Father Joseph
Katherina (Katya) Ivanovna Verkhovtskaia
Agrafena (Groushenka) Alexandrovna Svetka
A serving Girl
Arina
Stepanida

ACT I

The Hermitage of a Monastery near Moscow. A parlor giving on the cell of the Starets Zossima. At the rear an open gallery through which the flowering gardens of the Monastery are visible. One gets down there by a wooden stairway. To the left an entrance to a chapel. To the right a door leading to Father Zossima's cell. It's the end of the month of August, a beautiful afternoon—warm and clear.

AT RISE, the stage is empty. But father Zossima appears in the garden. He's an old man, small waist, thin and slightly bent over.

He walks very slowly and with difficulty and leans on the shoulder of Alyosha. Both mount the stairway. Reaching the last step Father Zossima stops to get his breath. In the distance voices singing a hymn.

Alyosha

(Listening to the singing) All those who come to you full of trouble leave appeased and satisfied.

Zossima

If it is permitted to a man, to a sinner, to thus rejoice the heart of his brothers, what can we not expect of God himself?

Alyosha

Father! How are you able to accomplish these marvels?

Zossima

Everything comes from God, my son. (takes several steps towards his cell then stops again) Alyosha, my child, I'm not too heavy for your shoulder? You see, from day to day my strength abandons me. I'm soon going to die.

(Alyosha silently places his face against the breast of the old man) Well,—don't cry. Death ought to rejoice us.

Alyosha

Will you leave me alone in the world?

Zossima

Life is beginning for you. The time has come.

Alyosha

I thought you were better today. Your face is smiling.

Zossima

(Starting to walk again) That woman who trekked six versts on foot with her child in her arms to bring me her offering gave me pleasure! Man is created for goodness, Alyosha—Be gay, be gay like children, like the birds of the sky. It suffices to love without cease, to love everybody—

(They reach the door of his cell. Alyosha raises his eyes which he kept lowered)

Alyosha

Near you everything is easy for me. Without you it's anguish and shadows.

Zossima

(Smiling) Well, you will go towards the shadows after my death.

(Alyosha bows, then kisses the hand of the Starets who blesses him and goes into his cell. Alyosha remains for a moment before the door, then heads toward the stairway, goes down the steps, then, noticing Dimitri, returns rapidly)

Dimitri

Alyosha. Do I frighten you?

Alyosha

(Going back down and extending his hand) Dimitri.

Dimitri

My little brother. (Songs of the pilgrims rise again in the distance)

Alyosha

(With increasing exaltation) Listen. It's the pilgrims withdrawing. They've just come from all over Russia. This morning we've had two miracles! First of one possessed. I saw Father Zossima place his stole on his head. It appeased him. Ah, brother, he's the greatest of men on earth, and I dwell in his house. I am present at his glory.

Dimitri

There are so many humiliated among men. Yes, in humiliation man suffers greatly on earth. I think only of that.

Alyosha

I love men.

Dimitri

But you flee them.

Alyosha

I believe in them. I flee temptations and filthy degradations.

Dimitri

Yes, the filthy degradations of your family.

Alyosha

Don't joke, Mitia. I'm capable of terrifying myself.

Dimitri

(Harshly) And you are taking care of your own salvation, my little monk.

Alyosha

It is said "share everything and follow me, if you desire perfection".

I intend to live for immortality.

Dimitri

That's fair! We need a saint to save The Karamazov's.

Alyosha

(Lowering his eyes) I am, like you, a Karamazov.

Dimitri

And you are still a virgin at twenty! (Alyosha turns away) Lyosha, my pigeon, don't turn away. Let me press you in my arms, because, truly, in the whole world, I love only you. (He pulls Alyosha, then raises his head and looks at him) I love you because you are perfectly pure and because you always tell the truth. Alexei, man of God, you, that we all love, don't you know that we all need you?

Alyosha

Ivan needs no one. He's seeking something. My youth and my ignorance make him smile. And of you, brother, I said to myself "He is saved!"—when I learned of your engagement to Katherina Ivanovna.

Dimitri

Yes, leaving the army. I was thinking of returning home with my fiancée to surround the old age of my father with attentions—and I found only a filthy debauchee—an ignoble mountebank.

Alyosha

Mitia—he's our father.

Dimitri

A father without feelings and modesty who made my mother die, and then yours, of shame and chagrin; an Aesop, a Pierrot, a skirt chaser.

Alyosha

We must pity him and forgive.

Dimitri

One cannot forgive a creature like that. Ivan said to me "You cannot forgive."

Alyosha

Don't listen to Ivan.

Dimitri

Why?

Alyosha

Ivan is an enigma.

Dimitri

An enigma, yes.

Alyosha

A mind always preoccupied with difficult thoughts—you know what thoughts—

Dimitri

He ought to straighten out everything between father and me. And now he excites me to hate him, which doesn't prevent him from living comfortably with him.

Alyosha

That is strange.

Dimitri

Everything is obscure, terrifying, incomprehensible. Lyosha, you will enlighten me; I intend to confess to you. Look, aren't you shocked by my face?

Alyosha

I see terror—I see joy.

Dimitri

I want to begin my confession with the hymn of Schiller—to joy! I have never been lower. But however ignoble and cursed I am, I am still your son, Lord! And I love you and joy is in me.

Alyosha

Glory to the Eternal in heaven.

Dimitri

Glory to the Eternal in me!—Come, sit down there, so I can see you! Don't say anything. I'm the one who will speak. But in whispers, I must speak in whispers—so that no one can hear me. Ah, Lyosha, why since this morning and all these recent days did I desire to see you? It's because you are necessary to me. It's necessary that a sublime soul pardon me. To you alone I intend to tell everything.—And you will listen to me without laughing. Tomorrow, a new life is going to begin for me.

Alyosha

Yes, brother, Katherina Ivanovna—

Dimitri

You know those dreams in which one falls off a cliff? Well, at his moment, it's as if I were falling without dreaming. Oh, I'm not afraid. Meaning, yes, I am afraid but that fear is sweet to me. Or rather, it's not sweet, it's intoxication. Is it that of beauty, the ideal? What enigmas. I have considered a lot, you know; for a Karamazov there's beauty even in shame. God, the mere idea of God makes me ill—And then who cares! See the beautiful Sun, the pure heaven, the green trees. We are in full summer. It's calm. What am I trying to say? I don't know.

Alyosha

Your fiancée.

Dimitri

(Softly with distress) Ah, yes Katherina—She tortures me Alyosha. I intend to break up with her.

Alyosha

You intend to abandon Katherina Ivanovna?

Dimitri

Don't pity her! She does what she wants; someone else will marry her, someone better than me.

Alyosha

Someone else?

Dimitri

Ivan, perhaps—

Alyosha

You are mad.

Dimitri

I believe he loves her. So much the better. Let him deliver me.

Alyosha

Oh, brother.

Dimitri

Great! You don't know anything yet and you scorn me. Do you imagine I can detach myself from her without being torn up? I wanted, I, too, wanted to raise myself up. All my life I've suffered from this thirst for nobility. I had, like you, my innocence, a heart avid for beauty! If you could see my heart.

Alyosha

Dimitri, I know that you will tell me the whole truth.

Dimitri

You want everything? Go, I won't withhold it. You know that I was a second lieutenant in a line Battalion. They treated me extra-ordinarily well in my little garrison village. I squandered money everywhere. They thought I was rich—besides I thought I was going to be. Then with my name entered in the battalion, it was rumored in the village of the coming arrival of the second daughter of the Colonel. She had just finished her studies in an aristocratic pensione in the Capital. Yes, Katherina Ivanovna—passed for a perfect beauty. One evening, at the home of the commandant of the battery, I approached her: she measured me with a look. Oh—I couldn't endure her scornful little smirk.

Alyosha

You loved her already?

Dimitri

I swear to you I felt she was so far above me. I'd understood that Katherina was not a kid, that she had character, pride, a solid virtue, and plenty of intelligence and education. Because of that, perhaps, I wanted to punish her for nor having understood what a man I am.

Alyosha

You detested her then?

Dimitri

I didn't know how to touch, to disturb this woman, so pure and so haughty. Right away, I felt the harm I was going to do her—and I couldn't prevent myself from doing it. Then, at that moment, I received 6,000 roubles from Father. And, almost at the same time, I learned through the indiscretion of a friend, that our Colonel, Katherina's father, was suspected of embezzlement. I arranged to meet the sister of Katherina Ivanovna, and to say to her, like this, in conversation "If by chance, they ask for your father's accounts and he cannot give them, instead of passing him to the Council, and to spare him the degradation, just send your sister to me. I have money I will give him the sum and no one will know a thing". It was a question of 4,500 roubles. The little one insulted me, but she carried my proposal to Katherina. That was all that I wanted. Soon a new Major arrived to take command of the detachment. As for me, I waited.

(A silence) Lyosha, two days later, at my home, evening fell. I was going to going out when suddenly, the door opened, and before me, in my chamber, appeared Katherina Ivanovna. No one had met her. It could remain a secret between us. She came in, her face shone with determination, insolence, even.—But I saw her lips were trembling. "My sister told me that you would give 4,500 roubles if I came to get them myself. Here I am. Give them to me." And she could not say more, her voice abruptly faded—Alyosha—are you listening? One would say you are sleeping.

Alyosha

I am listening.

Dimitri

My first thought was that of a Karamazov. I stared at Katherina. She was really beautiful, but at that moment, there was something in her that surpassed her beauty. She was coming to sacrifice herself for her father—and to me. She was in my hands body and soul. Do you understand? She was braving me. I was unable to control myself. Evil boiled within me. The more I felt myself unworthy of her—the more I wanted to do the vilest thing I was capable of. For a few minutes I examined her with a frightful hate!

Alyosha

Get to the point, get to the point!

Dimitri

I went to the window—I leaned my head against the icy glass. It seemed to me the cold burned me. Then, turning, I took 4,500 roubles from my drawer. Silently. I showed them to her, I folded them, I gave them to her—I opened the door myself, and I bowed very low—She trembled stared at me, went pale, pale—and suddenly, without speaking, but with a sweet glow, she prostrated herself before me, face to the ground.

Alyosha

(Not controlling an enthusiastic emotion) Brother, brother.

Dimitri

Then she got up rapidly and fled. And as for me, after she left, I pulled my saber from its sheath to kill myself—without knowing why—from enthusiasm. You understand—say that it's possible to kill oneself through enthusiasm.

Alyosha

Brother, at that moment you had raised yourself higher than she herself and you had conquered her.

Dimitri

Not bad, novice! You said the word: Yes in that instant, only in that instant, me—a camp follower of an officer, I conquered the little lady! And it's that, you see—what she'll never forgive me for, because she is proud. Later her father died, she paid his debt to me. But that's not enough. She decided, from gratitude, to sacrifice her life to me. What she calls her gratitude is a need to dominate, it's an infinite thirst with which she is devoured. She resembles me, Alyosha, nothing will be able to stop her.

Alyosha

When she left you that day, you loved her?

Dimitri

I really loved my beautiful deed, and as for her, she was humiliated—

Alyosha

After that you became engaged?

Dimitri

Three months later—before the Holy Images—Ah, would I could erase that day from my life. The day, Alyosha, the day when she told me that she loved me, the day when she wrote me—I kept her letter—and I will never let it go. I want to be buried with it. You will read it, I am unworthy, with my besmirched voice, to repeat those words. She gave me an incurable wound. (He lowers his head and weeps)

Alyosha

(Tenderly) Mitia, you are wretched, but you mustn't despair.

Dimitri

Why did I put my saber back in its furrow? I ought to have killed myself that same evening, since I was going to fall back. I tried to explain this to her in a letter, at the time of our engagement. That, and many other things, she didn't want to understand. That was when I sent Ivan to her. I thought that he could persuade her better than I could, that it was folly to get engaged to each other.

Alyosha

But you told me—

Dimitri

Yes, Ivan was taken with her. She loves him, too, I'm sure of it, but she says nothing. She has submitted to his charm—Why wouldn't they love each other? She, so pure—he, so intelligent. It was necessary.

Alyosha

But you, what will you do?

Dimitri

(With anger) I'll go back to my mud. (A silence)

Alyosha

My poor brother.

Dimitri

Shut up. Don't pity me!

Alyosha

(With authority) You love Katherina. By renouncing her, by sacrificing yourself, I am sure you are punishing yourself for a sin that is not irreparable. Stop defending yourself against me. You haven't told me everything yet.

Dimitri

I want to distance myself from her—that's all.

Alyosha

You were weeping just now.

Dimitri

Stupidities! I'm strong because I've made a decision.

Alyosha

(With anguish) Mitia?

Dimitri

Oh—fear nothing, little brother. I won't kill myself. I don't have the strength now. Later, perhaps. But not before having—enough! I won't say anymore—I'm leaving—What time is it?

Alyosha

Eleven o'clock, I think.

Dimitri

Goodbye. Don't pray for me—it's useless. (Starts to leave but stops, takes his brother's hands in his and looks at him in silence) Are you still able to love me, Alexei? I have ferocious passions—I'm violent, sensual, I love debauchery and its cruelty. But whatever I've done and may yet do, nothing equals the infamy that I'm bearing now, here, in my breast. Say, do you imagine that Dimitri Karamazov could be a thief, a dirty little thief?—The day before yesterday, Katherina Ivanovna took me mysteriously, I don't know why—to dispatch to her sister Agafa, in Moscow, 3,000 roubles that she entrusted me with. I didn't have a kopeck, Katherina knew it. Still, she confided this cursed money to me. She smiled when she gave it to me. Why did she smile? I took it! I went to the post office. I didn't go in.

Alyosha

(Out of breath) What has become of the money, Dimitri? What has become of the money?

Dimitri

(Low striking his breast) It's here. I carry it here, wrapped in a package on my breast. I haven't touched it. Not yet. That's what's atrocious, Lyosha, I'm not yet a thief, since I haven't yet spent the money. But I won't be able to prevent myself from doing it. Unless there's a miracle, I won't be able to.

Alyosha

(Violently) Give me that money!

Dimitri

My father has defrauded me more than 6,000 roubles from my mother's inheritance. Let him give me 3,000 and I will hold him quits. He must give them to me! If not, I am ruined. I cannot get out of it otherwise. I'll do no matter what. Dimitri Karamazov has conceived this base calculation: 3,000 roubles, cost for cost. If the old man gives them, good. I remain an honest man—If he refuses, I'm keeping Katherina's money and I am a thief. And behold I am suspended over the abyss. Will I be hurled into the night of shame, or will I mount to light and joy? Interesting, isn't it? Bah! I am already damned because I've thought of it.

Alyosha

Why did you have this thought? Why have you kept these 3,000 roubles?

Dimitri

Why! Why! It had to be. Am I not an evil worm? The worthy son of my father? In our family, sensuality goes as far as madness. Goodbye! You will learn all about it later. The abyss, the night, no need to explain it all to you. Mud and Hell! Don't question me further! Nothing pure before me, get out of my way. Let me leave! (Seeing Smerdiakov climbing the stairs) Eh! The Lackey. Smerdiakov—! What's wrong with him?

Smerdiakov

(Lowering deeply) Sir, I salute you.

Dimitri

What's happened? Why did you leave your post?

Smerdiakov

Sir, excuse me, I knew I'd find you here.

Dimitri

Cease with ceremonies! The news!

Smerdiakov

Can I speak with you privately for a moment?

Dimitri

Speak before my brother.

Smerdiakov

I don't know if I ought. Sir, this news is confidential.

Dimitri

Stay put, Alyosha.

Smerdiakov

News of great importance.

Dimitri

Will you speak, stinking, impudent lackey!

Smerdiakov

Of—if you are going to be angry.

Dimitri

(Seizing him by the shoulder) I'll break your bones.

Smerdiakov

Yi, yi—Sir, don't hurt me, sir, you are frightening me. Here—here—

Dimitri

You are doing this intentionally to irritate me.

Smerdiakov

Well, sir, I believe I have, Alas! strong reasons to believe that your father is on the verge of carrying her off. (Violent gesture by Dimitri) Wait at least to the end of my report, Dimitri Feodorovitch, and don't cast such terrifying looks at me. I say that a danger threatens you—Groushenka, who, recently seemed in the best disposition toward you, has abruptly turned to favor Feodor Pavlovitch .

Dimitri

She told you that?

Smerdiakov

This morning my master received a letter from Groushenka. You could almost see blood rising to the head of your father as he read it.

Dimitri

(Spitting) Filth!

Smerdiakov

I don't know by what means he was able to vanquish her resistance and overcome her hesitation, but it is certain that, without giving him a formal assurance, she is allowing your father to hope that she will come to his place this very evening.

Dimitri

At what time?

Smerdiakov

Midnight.

Dimitri

You've read the letter?

Smerdiakov

I've read it.

Dimitri

You're the one who betrayed me, vermin.

Smerdiakov

Would I be coming immediately to warn you?

Dimitri

What's the old man doing?

Smerdiakov

Feodor Pavlovitch is preparing to receive the young lady! I had heard him beg your brother Ivan to leave this evening for his property of Tchermachnia, so as to complete, he said, a sale of wood. In reality it's so as not to be troubled by his presence. Even worse, just now he was preparing a package of thirty one-hundred-rouble notes, bound with a red ribbon and sealed—on which he wrote "To my angel, Groushenka, if she deigns to come."

Dimitri

You've seen the money?

Smerdiakov

Three thousand roubles. Your father showed them to me before hiding them under his mattress.

Dimitri

The old Tom Cat seduces girls with money which belongs to me! (Turning towards Alyosha) Ah, ah! You are there, you, eyes wide open! Do you understand now? This Groushenka that my father's trying to choke me with it's with her that I intend to leave, it's for her that I want the money. In my return from the regiment they told me my father was smitten with this girl, wanted to make her his heir, and that it was because of her that he was refusing me the money he owed me. I ran to the home of Groushenka. I was going to beat her up!

Alyosha

You love her!

Dimitri

Do you imagine that I got nothing from her, not at all. The old man, neither. He hasn't got her yet. She's slippery like a snake.

Alyosha

Still—If Groushenka goes to father's house this evening—

Dimitri

I will enter by force and I will prevent it!

Alyosha

And if—?

Dimitri

If? I—I won't endure it.

Alyosha

Mitia!

Dimitri

I don't know. I don't know what I will do! I fear his cursed face. His double chin, his nose, his bold smile disgusts me so much that I cannot control myself.

Smerdiakov

Ah, sir, what are you saying?

Dimitri

If you let her into my father's home without warning me, I will kill you first.

Smerdiakov

(Squirming) No danger for the moment. Your father and your brother will arrive at the monastery after me.

Dimitri

At the monastery? What to do?

Smerdiakov

Feodor Pavlovitch has got it in his head to submit to the Reverend Father Zossima the quarrel that divides you regarding the inheritance of your poor late mother Adelaida Mioussov. He insists that the situation and the personality of the monk are of a nature to impose an accord.

Dimitri

What new buffoonery is this?

Alyosha

Brother, I fear some scandal! (Smerdiakov leaves)

Dimitri

He intends to intimidate me: so be it! I will speak out before the monk. He will actually be the one to give up. And after that, I'll rush to Groushenka and carry her off. We will be happy far from all this. You, brother, you will go to the home of Katherina.

Alyosha

Go there yourself and take her the money.

Dimitri

And if, soon, Groushenka tells me "Take me, I'm yours"?

Alyosha

You must confess everything to Katherina. It's your salvation.

Dimitri

So she will pardon me, right? So she can hold me under her heel? I don't want her sacrifices. Let Ivan marry her! They are worthy of each other and everything will be put straight. I bless them. But Groushenka! My Groushenka become the prey of this old slime! I love Groushenka! She's a real woman. She doesn't hold my vices against me. We will fight.

But we will love each other. She's the only one I can love. I intend to marry Groushenka! I cannot live without her.

Alyosha

You are ruining yourself, Mitia. But God knows your heart; he sees your despair! He won't allow atrocious things to take place. You won't betray sacred engagements. (Ivan followed by Smerdiakov appears at the top of the stairs)

Ivan

(Interrupting Alyosha) Bravo, novice! You preach well!

Alyosha

(Blushing) You always are making fun, Vania.

Ivan

No rancor, little brother. I love to tease you a bit. It amuses me to see your eyes sparkle. Hello, Mitia! Still wild?

Dimitri

Hello, Ivan, dear brother. Be happy.

Alyosha

Ivan, you knew everything and you didn't tell me.

Dimitri

He's secret like the tomb.

Alyosha

(To Ivan) You are separating yourself from us?

Ivan

I'm going to let you chat.

Dimitri

Listen. If two beings succeed in rising above terrestrial things—if not both, at least one of them—The one who's going to disappear comes to the other and says, "Do for me this or that" things that one asks only on one's death bed, can the one who remains refuse to obey, if he's a friend or a brother?

Ivan

What a way to talk. Where are you coming from? Speak more clearly.

Dimitri

(Struggling against his emotions) Right after leaving here, go to Katherina Ivanovna's—greet her on my behalf and tell her that she will never see me again.

Ivan

Are you losing your mind?

Dimitri

Don't be harsh. I am speaking solemnly. You know Katherina. You know what she wants. You know what I am. She esteems you for your intelligence, she respects you for the purity of your life. She has confidence in you and you have power over her. Make her understand, once and for all, that she has no right to ruin her entire life under the pretext of gratitude which is absurd.

Ivan

Carry your message to her—Better take Alyosha for your ambassador.

Dimitri

You're the one I've chosen, Ivan. You will tell her "Dimitri sent me" She will understand.

Ivan

(Turning away) What a comedy! (Feodor can be heard chatting and laughing in the garden)

Alyosha

Here's father!

Dimitri

Do you hear him laughing? Come, Alyosha.

Alyosha

Let's go into the chapel. Till later, Ivan. (Alyosha and Dimitri go into the chapel)

Ivan

Well, what are you doing there?

Smerdiakov

Nothing, sir, I'm thinking.

Ivan

May I know about what?

Smerdiakov

Why—all this

Ivan

And—what do you think about it?

Smerdiakov

Ah, sir, your father and your brother make me uneasy. They are more and more on this narrow path. Will they know how to control themselves?

Ivan

(Between his teeth) We will see.

Smerdiakov

It's a pity, sir, that a young gentleman like your brother Dimitri should abandon his fiancée like this. Not to mention that Katherina Ivanovna is rich now. Her aunt in Moscow has endowed her.

Ivan

(Looking sideways) You know that, too?

Smerdiakov

Fifty thousand roubles. Sir, that's not so shabby for a lad who has nothing. It's a handsome share you know! (Lowering his voice a bit) And at a sign from Groushenka, your brother will give it all up—

Ivan

Is that any business of yours?

Smerdiakov

He's rushing to his ruin!

Ivan

And that afflicts a good Christian like you?

Smerdiakov

Wouldn't you be afflicted by it?

Ivan

Dimitri is my brother.

Smerdiakov

I think I'm sort of part of the family. Do you know, that being drunk last week, Dimitri Feodorovitch proclaimed himself unworthy of his fiancée Katherina before a whole tavern? He will end by tiring her. (In confidence) She's already hesitating—

Feodor

(At the back, speaking to two monks) Yet another sign of the cross, gentlemen—everywhere you turn. (With great affectation he makes signs of the cross before two icons, then turns) Eh, dear Ivan! These monks live in a vale of roses!

Ivan

(In a low voice) Father, I warn you—if you don't control yourself here, I am going to leave you, and right away.

Feodor

What did I say wrong? For a free-thinker, you seem pretty well tormented by your sins. Are you afraid the saintly reader of thoughts won't decipher from your eyes what's going on behind your face?

(He laughs; Ivan moves away shrugging his shoulders)

Smerdiakov

(Going to Feodor) Sir,—your son Dimitri is here. Hush! I don't know how he got wind of this meeting. It's frightful to listen to him. Be calm, sir, I beg you—some dignity.

Feodor

Don't leave me.

Smerdiakov

Don't worry. (The two monks have gone to announce the visitors. Alyosha returns from the chapel)

Feodor

Ah, here he is, here he is! (Runs to hug Alyosha) Dear and good child, come to my arms! My little pigeon, I intend to give you my paternal blessing. No: I'm only going to make the sign of the cross to you. There! My Alyosha! Are you happy here? There are no women, I think. Or—oh—at least have you prayed for the rest of us sinners? We sin a lot down here, you know. I always said to myself "Who then will pray for me?" Because, you see, dear lad, I am not strong up there, no! That doesn't prevent me from thinking about it, sometimes. Not always—Oh, oh, oh, I am scandalizing you, poor pigeon? Do you think I want to cheapen you? Go, go, my little one, remain in your monastery, you will always be better off there than with an old drunk and a bunch of skirt chasers, although nothing touches you. You are an angel. And for all that, you are not stupid, you've chosen the best role! So then, if ever you find the truth here, come tell it to me, huh? The departure for the next world will be easier for me if I know surely what's taking place there. I've never met anyone yet who could give me any information about it. Come on, you will burn, you will burn yourself out, you will be cured and one day you will return to the unfortunate old man no one loves. (Weeping) And as for me, I will wait for you, because you alone in the world don't blame me, my dear lad.

Alyosha

Father—

Feodor

(Swallowing his tears) Fine, it's finished. Where is he, your reverend father? We all come to prostrate ourselves before him—Smerdiakov understands that? You've recognized our delightful Smerdiakov? He always has the pretty face and distinction of a eunuch, eh? And what elegance—varnished boots. He's studying philosophy now, you know. Yes, Ivan is giving him lessons. He's Ivan's disciple. (Lower pointing to the back where Ivan and Smerdiakov are chatting) Heavens, look at the jolly couple they make. And this Ivan, what a look he gives me! Alyosha, you mustn't love Ivan.

Ivan

Stop outraging my brother.

Feodor

Ivan isn't one of us. He doesn't have our soul.

Alyosha

I saw Dimitri just now.

Feodor

Your Dimitri! I'll make him crack under my slipper like a cockroach. I know that you love him—but that doesn't worry me. If Ivan loved him then I'd be afraid. Luckily, Ivan doesn't love anyone. Ivan's not a man like us. (Two monks appear)

Alyosha

(Greatly worried) Father, father—father Zossima's going to come. I wanted to ask you—to beg you—you must consider his great age—and his weak health, the sanctity of this place, the gravity of the circumstances—

Feodor

Why certainly, the sanctity. Evidently I'll consider it. Do you think me evil?

Alyosha

I don't believe you evil, but you are not in control of yourself. (Father Zossima appears. Ivan and Smerdiakov go to each other…to Ivan) Brother I have confidence in you. (Going to Father Zossima) (The two monks bow to Father Zossima who returns their greetings. Supported by Alyosha, he comes forward, Smerdiakov, Ivan and Feodor, behind them, bowing)

Feodor

(After a silence, bows anew to Zossima, stammering) Holy old man—! What emotion.

Zossima

Sit down, gentlemen.

Feodor

(Bowing and murmuring) Thanks, thanks—a very great sinner, no doubt about it, very unworthy—

Zossima

Don't worry about that—

Feodor

No, no—I'll be quiet—with gratitude. (Starting) Not without having—at first, nevertheless, cleared up certain doubts—venerable Father, that the habit of confessing men has given you the extra-ordinary power to divine at first glance the moral tortures that afflict them? No, right? Exaggerated? Very exaggerated? My son Ivan, just now seemed to take this legend seriously and my word frightened himself! (Ivan comes up to him to say something that cannot be heard) What? No? It's not true? Fine. Good. So be it! I didn't say anything. (Heatedly) Alas, Master! You have before you a talkative old fellow, a real buffoon, that's how I present myself.

Zossima

Don't be ashamed of yourself—danger comes from it.

Feodor

Very true! It always seems to me when I take some decision, that I am more vile than all the others, and that one must take me for a true buffoon. In that case I'll joke around! Very true! But with a temperament like that, I'm really worried about never getting to an eternal life.

Zossima

You'll get to it, little by little. You must leave the bottle, hold your tongue, be chaste and not love money too much. Above all, don't lie.

Feodor

(Throwing himself on his knees and striking his breast) I am lies, the father of lies, and the son of lies. But you have enlightened me!

Zossima

Get up. This is yet another gesture of a liar.

Feodor

(Completely disconcerted) Pardon me, holy Father, excuse my trouble! You see, it's because I have a little doubt, in recent times. My dear son Ivan, since he's done me the honor of living under my roof, enjoys waving certain questions before me.

Ivan

I've never waved questions before you.

Feodor

So be it! In that case I will say you don't wave them, but he poses them, these questions, like charades, enigmas. And then he backs off and plays the philosopher, he plays with my poor mind.

Zossima

(To Ivan) I pity you, sir.

Ivan

(Smiling politely) Why do you pity me?

Zossima

Because you have not yet resolved the problem and it must be resolved.

Ivan

(Still politely) Is there a resolution?

Zossima

May God dictate it to you in time. May he help you and bless your noble suffering.

Feodor

Meanwhile—with all these ideas that are circulating. It must be confessed that calm faith no longer dwells by my hearth. (Pointing to Alyosha) Since that angel left it! They think too much, around me, that bothers me. Yes, even my lackey. Didn't this Jesuit come to ask me how light was created on the fourth day since the stars were created first? Then, my faith, which wasn't very solid, was in danger from hour to hour, I swear it. This question of lackeys has been the origin and the cause of all my moral abasement! (To Ivan who, beside himself, heads toward the door) Well, my dear son, what are you doing? Don't go away! I'm finished. I'm coming to the question which brings us here. Ah—here it is: Holy Father, be judge. Dimitri Feodorovitch my disrespectful son, the shame of my old age, is demanding 3,000 roubles from me. They accuse me of having hidden money from my children in my boots and refused them their due. But I have wherewith to reply. I have all the documents establishing what this young man possessed, and what he spent and what remains to him. It's vain for the whole world to be against me. Dimitri, remains my debtor and not for a bagatelle. (Dimitri emerges from the chapel and goes calmly, hat in hand to Father Zossima)

Dimitri

(Respectfully) As for me, I've never understood anything of the account that my father furnished me. But I affirm—

Feodor

Do you believe in the word of such a savage? All they talk about in the town are his debauches. Down there, in the regiment, he spent a couple thousand roubles at the same time to seduce honest girls.

Dimitri

(Controlling himself) You are acting badly towards me father. I know what feeling is driving you on.

Feodor

Haven't you been bewitched by a young lady, the daughter of his former Colonel? He dishonored her and now—

Dimitri

I won't allow you to slander in my presence the most noble woman in the world. And I do not want for anything to be in the scandal you are causing in such a place and before such venerable persons. I prefer to withdraw.

Feodor

Ah, Mitia, Mitia, what will you do if I give you to take with you, my paternal curse—what will you do?

Dimitri

(Raising his voice) I'm the one who curses you!

Feodor

To his father! To his father!

Dimitri

(Striding toward Feodor) All the evil has come to us from you. You've infected your soul and our life. I swear, gentlemen, that I wouldn't have said a single word against him. But, since he insults me, I'm going to unveil his turpitudes, even though he may be my father.

Feodor

Dimitri Feodorovitch if you weren't my son, I'd provoke you to a duel at three feet, across a handkerchief!

Alyosha

(To Ivan) Brother, prevent them—

Dimitri

Your son! Have you ever treated me like a son? My mother was hardly dead—I wasn't even two, when you "forgot me" in the home of your concierge where I was devoured by fleas. And after that—Ivan, Alexei, if you are unaware of it, well, I saw it, this man brought prostitutes to his home and organized orgies there right before the eyes of Sophie Ivanovna, your mother.

Alyosha

(Pulling Ivan's arm) Ivan—Ivan.

Dimitri

Hold on (Seeing Smerdiakov he grabs him and brings him forward terrified) This sick chicken, this epileptic snail—I present to you Smerdiakov—my brother, yes—the real son of Feodor Pavlovitch who made him his lackey. He had him with La Puante an idiot beggar woman who he besmirched while she slept in a ditch by the road.

Monks

Enough, enough, intolerable (They murmur)

Dimitri

Let it go that he's my brother—I don't care. But you, Ivan, who have great aspirations—you, Alyosha, who seek God, Smerdiakov is your brother! Look at him! (He releases Smerdiakov who trembles and moves away)

Feodor

(Fist raised toward Dimitri) Kick him out, kick him out.

Dimitri

Ah, you are really crowning your life, father. Sooner than release a Kopeck, you prefer that your son be reduced to theft.

Feodor

I owe you nothing, nothing.

Dimitri

And you outrage with your lusts the woman that I love. You flatter yourself you'll take Groushenka away from me, right? You are expecting her tonight.

Feodor

(Recoiling) She's chosen me. I'll marry her if I like.

Dimitri

Shut up!

Feodor

Watch over your Katherina. You will find her docile to your caprices—these pale and tender young girls don't love debauchees and rogues! (Dimitri without replying throws himself on his father, fist raised) Defend me, defend me! He's going to kill me. (Feodor escapes shouting. Dimitri runs after him)

Ivan

(Intervening, barring Dimitri's path) Stop. Fool!

Dimitri

(Trembling under the hand of his brother) What is the use of a life of such a creature? (Everyone is on their feet. General stupefaction, Father Zossima advances slowly toward Dimitri, and suddenly prostrates himself at his feet. Shocked, Dimitri covers his face with his hands and then looks around him) Why? Why? Now it's all over. Come on everything is over. (Starts to go to the stairway, the goes back and calls Ivan) Ivan! Don't forget about Katherina. This very day you will pay your respects to her—you will pay your respects to her. (He runs out down the stairs)

Feodor

(To the monks) That's fine, gentlemen, that's fine, I'm leaving, I'm withdrawing—I may be a buffoon, but I am a gentlemen. (He leaves. The monks follow him) (Father Zossima is still kneeling. Alyosha bends over him. Ivan stays at the right, Smerdiakov goes to him)

Smerdiakov

Sir, what signifies this bow to the ground?

Ivan

I don't worry my head guessing at enigmas.

Smerdiakov

If you hadn't held him back, sir, he would have killed him.

Ivan

Who cares! One swine eats another—they get what they deserve.

Alyosha

(Raising his head, stops Ivan from leaving) Brother, do you believe that one man has the right to decide if another man is worthy of living or not?

Ivan

(Haughtily) The questions you ask!

Alyosha

You must reply, Ivan.

Ivan

What's the use of lying? If a man is made this way, what can I do? If all desires are permitted?

Alyosha

All desires—

Ivan

Yes—who does not have the right to desire?

Alyosha

Even the death of another?

Ivan

(Impatiently) Do you believe. I am capable, like Dimitri, of killing the old goat? Huh?

Alyosha

What are you saying, Ivan? Neither you, nor Dimitri! I never thought so.

Ivan

In that case, why are you blushing? (Tapping Alyosha's cheek) Calm down, little one. I will always protect father, as I did just now.

Alyosha

Ah—

Ivan

As for my desires, I allow them complete freedom. (Meanwhile Father Zossima's gotten back up. He considers Alyosha with a deep emotion that prevents him from speaking. Then he presses Alyosha silently against his breast.)

Zossima

Your place is no longer here, my son. It is time to go be with your brothers. Not one of them, but both. Why do you tremble?

Alyosha

Because I am afraid. This bow—before Dimitri?

Zossima

I bowed to his great suffering—that soon will come. Hurry!

Alyosha

(Fearfully) I prefer this calm monastery. I love you, my father.

Zossima

Alyosha, your heart has spent itself enough in ecstasy. Goodbye—because not only my days but my hours are limited. (Zossima has slowly pulled Alyosha toward the stairs. Once there, he frees himself from him)

Alyosha

(Kissing the hands of the monk) Goodbye. Goodbye. (Alyosha begins to descend the stairs, face turned toward Father Zossima who leans toward him)

Zossima

(At the last moment, going down a step, hands stretched toward Alyosha, in a low voice, as if speaking confidentially) Alyosha, if ever you can take on yourself the crime of another—suffer for him and let him leave without reproach. Go, my cherished son, go. (Alyosha in tears moves away. Father Zossima blesses him, and once he's in the garden still follows him with his eyes, for a long while leaning on the balustrade)

CURTAIN

ACT II

The afternoon of the same day. The home of Katherina Ivanovna. An elegantly furnished boudoir. A window on the left. A door in the rear leading to a vestibule. Door to the right, and one on the left leading to Katherina's room.

AT RISE, Katherina, dressed in black, is seated by a table which she leans on, face in her hands, seemingly obstinate, very pale. Ivan paces back and forth. It's evident that a conversation between them has been interrupted by Ivan's violence. He stops pacing and looks at Katherina. He goes to her and leans on the table which separates them.

Ivan

(In a low but shaking voice) It's sad, Katherina, that you don't feel the need to be happy.

Katherina

(Shaking her head) I know something more imperious than happiness.

Ivan

(Standing up with a smile) Duty!

Katherina

Superior to duty and which attracts me—

Ivan

Love of danger, curiosity of chance. All that wounds your heart seems to exalt your will. You don't feel alive unless risking your life.

Katherina

Because life is not beautiful enough.

Ivan

(Going back to her) You cannot yet know how powerful it is. It drags you—

Katherina

I will pray to God that He assist me.

Ivan

Your God! One can do what He asks, only by possessing dreadful gifts.

Katherina

All trials will find me prepared and can only rejoice me.

Ivan

While you wait for I don't know what reward! But suppose there is no reward. If there is no purpose? One knows nothing.

Katherina

One can believe.

Ivan

So be it! I believe, I admit—And meanwhile? It's your life passing, your life—happiness and joy on earth.

Katherina

(Almost harshly) You don't understand suffering.

Ivan

Would you know it in a longer time? And if you need ten years, fifteen years to use up your inhuman resistance to accepting your real feelings—if you admit, too late, that life such as it is—is worth more if you return towards it. Ah, Katherina you will have consumed your youth, the most beautiful time, at a time when everything was possible! You will have spent it—in a struggle, with this boaster—with this madman.

Katherina

(Rising) I will soon defeat Dimitri.

Ivan

You will ruin yourself with him.

Katherina

I will rescue him by the constancy of my love.

Ivan

He has refused your love.

Katherina

I will force his admiration. He won't be able to detach himself from me. I swore that to myself the day when, having me at his mercy, he so generously spared me. I alone saw him in that moment, the most beautiful of his life, I alone know what one can expect of him.

Ivan

Thus a momentary impression, a fugitive enthusiasm dictates to you the rule of an entire life. And you take for love this eternal duty. Now that's your folly.

Katherina

Do you think I'm capable of being cured of it?

Ivan

Katherina! You don't love your youth? You aren't really avid—I'm not speaking of happiness—but of fulfillment—of using your strength! Think! If the love of an equal—of a man worthy of you—if beautiful thoughts, the impetuous efforts that you squander today, found a way to spread, if they bore their fruit.

Katherine

(Very upset) Perhaps, yes, to think that he exists, perhaps—the one of whom you speak. That thought pleases me—but doesn't seduce me.

Ivan

You don't dare look at it.

Katherina

Rather, the more it seduces me, the more glorious I feel in loving Dimitri.

Ivan

Even unfaithful!

Katherina

I really want him to be weak.

Ivan

You accept that he loves another woman?

Katherina

He imagines he loves her.

Ivan

He's lustful. By thwarting his lusts you'll only irritate him.

Katherina

There's something noble in him that I will know how to address myself to.

Ivan

You will envenom the wounds of his soul. You will exasperate a frightful battle in his soul, in which that which is noble will not be able to sweep away that which is infamous.

Katherina

You've never spoken like this.

Ivan

Spare me making myself my brother's accuser before you.

Katherina

You haven't told me about anything I haven't forgiven in advance. For the last three days, I've been waiting for him. Wherever he may be I know what he's thinking. Whatever he may have done he must return to me. When he accuses himself, I will say to him—"I knew that." However long he delays. I won't await him with less confidence—

Ivan

(Cutting her short) Katherina, it's Dimitri who sent me.

Katherina

(Whose face has altered) Why's he sending you? What did he say? I want to know exactly.

Ivan

(Straight in her face) He ordered me to greet you—and to tell you he will never see you again.

Katherina

(Putting a good face on it) And then?

Ivan

That's all.

Katherina

Always the same! Greet me—That's the word he actually used.

Ivan

He actually insisted on that word.

Katherina

He was exalted, beside himself perhaps?

Ivan

I don't know any more.

Katherina

He was terrified by his decision. By stressing the word he intended to stress the bravado.

Ivan

That's possible.

Katherina

Does he imagine he is leaving me without response to his

greeting.

Ivan

Actually, I expect, to the contrary, that you would skewer this bravado with your most glorious reply.

Katherina

You don't think I'm sincere.

Ivan

Oh—to the worst excess, sincere even in lying!

Serving Girl

(Enters) Alexei Feodorovitch Karamazov asks if you can receive him.

Katherina

It's your brother, Ivan. I am ravished that he's come. (To servant) Show him in.

Serving Girl

There's also that lady that you—

Katherina

Fine! Fine—Put her in the salon. I will see her in a moment. (The servant leaves, Katherina goes to Ivan) Ivan Feodorovitch if you see clearly in me—with those piercing eyes you've got, I entreat you—if you are indeed the person I believe you to be, the person I admire, and who has helped me so many times.

I entreat you to continue to support me in the path I've laid out. I've suffered a lot. I'm ready to suffer yet more. It may be that one day I'll reproach myself for having disobeyed you. But I intend to go on to the end. I need all my strength and without you—what will become of me. (Ivan and Katherina are standing close to each other. Ivan lowers his head and his hand leans on a little table. Katherina has placed her hand on Ivan's. Alyosha envelops them with a look as he enters)

Alyosha

(Low, bowing) God be with you.

Katherina

(Going rapidly to him) Alexei Feodorovitch, Alyosha—you'll allow me to call you thus? I am so happy to see you.

Alyosha

(Looking alternatively at Ivan and Katherine) Excuse me, Miss. I feel that my visit is perhaps out of place. But I am so uneasy about my brother Dimitri, the danger that he's running is so great. Doubtless, my brother Ivan will have told you already—

Katherina

That Dimitri no longer wants to see me, yes—

Alyosha

I rushed to you because I thought that you alone could save him.

Katherina

Sit down, Alyosha. You are going to speak to me frankly, without bothering to spare me, what you think—of his disposition, after—all that's taken place these last days.

Alyosha

Oh—I understand no great thing about these affairs.

Katherina

Your word is the purest I can gather.

Alyosha

My brother has committed many sins. But he knows that he sins. He isn't evil. He loves God. He loves you. You entered deeply into his heart, like an arrow that he can no longer tear out. He loves you—and yet I think that you frightened him— You are his best thought—and that thought tortures him.

Katherina

Look, did he speak to you of a sum of money—of 3,000 roubles?

Alyosha

Ah, you know?

Katherina

I guessed that he didn't forward it to my sister. By confiding the money to him, I was testing him—

Ivan

There's the wager you made.

Alyosha

So that's the way you are seeking to humiliate him?

Katherina

I wanted to shame him—and that he come to me as to God—that he finally learn I am capable of all pardons.

Ivan

Well, he hasn't come.

Katherina

So he still doesn't know me yet?

Alyosha

Now that he's lost his honor nothing matters to him.

Katherina

Let him come! I will welcome him, I will console him.

Alyosha

Even knowing why he kept the money?

Katherina

To deceive me with that Groushenka, and to run away with her, right? And you think I am going to abandon the struggle because Dimitri is submitting to a passing whim? Because it's not love, you hear? He cannot love her!

Ivan

Still—

Katherina

Groushenka is a siren! That's what you are going to tell me. An irresistible woman—and I cannot even support her look?

Alyosha

She's perfidious and dangerous—

Katherina

We are going to see if this little girl of pleasure has more decision and strength than I do; if her charms are better than my love in knowing how to keep a noble heart, or if I will know how to make her release his heart. (Pointing to the door.) Groushenka is here. You are going to make her acquaintance.

Ivan

Katherina Ivanovna, I won't be present at this scene. Allow me to say goodbye to you.

Katherina

(Imperiously) Stay, Ivan Feodorovitch. I insist on it.

Ivan

(Sneering) Indeed, you are going to tame this wild animal.

Katherina

I've done more difficult things, trust me. (Opening the door) Agrafena Alexandrovna—we are impatient to see you!

Groushenka

(In a drawling voice before entering) Here I am Miss. I was waiting to be called. (Groushenka is all dolled up. Her smiling face is naïve and almost childish. She glides rather than walks, with small timid motions of her head)

Katherina

(Presenting) Ivan Feodorovitch (Groushenka curtsies, Ivan barely nods) Alexei Feodorovitch! (Groushenka looks at him with curiosity and makes a gesture with her head. Alyosha bows. Katherina gestures for Groushenka to sit, considers her for a moment, then with a little constraint, but with dignity) You didn't misinterpret, I hope, the oddness of my action. I wanted to know you. I thank you for having come.

Groushenka

(Affectedly) Oh, to thank me. Oh, it's I, Miss, who owe you gratitude because you have not disdained me.

Katherina

(Forcing herself) I don't think that you will often be disdained with a face like that. (To Ivan) You saw the beautiful hair.

Groushenka

(Smiling) You make me confused. But take care—if you flatter me like this I am going to be suspicious.

Katherina

(Whose voice trembles a little) I only want an honest explanation between us.

Groushenka

(With an abrupt hand gesture) Hush! (Pointing to the door) There's someone there. (Gets up rapidly)

Katherina

It's the maid.

Groushenka

Are you sure of it? They're not listening behind the door?

Katherina

Why what's wrong with you?

Groushenka

Hush! (Cocking her ear at the door and listening) I'm stupid! I thought it was Dimitri Feodorovitch coming over here; it seemed to me twice that I saw him. I cannot take a step without his spying on me. Oh, I'm afraid of him—You promise me he won't come?

Katherina

Look—

Groushenka

Then—I am satisfied. He mustn't find me! For the last three days I have escaped him. If he learned now that I lied—Ah, all would be lost—So many things have taken place that he mustn't know about. That's why you see me nervous. He could have set a trap for me. (The maid appears. She bears a platter with chocolate, cake and sweets)

Katherina

You will accept a cup of chocolate—some cakes? At least you like Champagne, yes?

Groushenka

I love chocolate. (The maid leaves, Katherina fills glasses)

Katherina

Sweets, you like them, too? I will serve you myself.

Groushenka

(Laughing cheerfully) It's too much, it's too much!

Katherina

Some cigarettes. (They light cigarettes) And—permit me to ask what are these—things of which you make such a mystery—to Dimitri?

Groushenka

(Falling back in the chair and chapping her hands) Ah! There we are! There we are! You are curious. I know quite well you are intrigued. And if it amuses me to make you languish now? (To Alyosha) That interests you, too. But these are not things to talk about before a young monk.

Katherina

You are making him blush—

Groushenka

It's well done! He turned away his eyes, a little while ago, when passing me on the stairway. I guessed it was he and I was furious—because I thought he scorned me. (To Alyosha who looks at her smiling) You are not intimidated? (Alyosha shakes his head) You'll extend your hand to me. (Alyosha extends his hand to her) I frighten you?

Alyosha

No, my sister.

Groushenka

How he said that! I don't know why, I am myself so content to see you.

Katherina

(Going to Groushenka) We are going to be friends.

Groushenka

(Still looking at Alyosha) His brother has often spoken to me of him. As for me, I'm vile—I thought "How such a man must scorn me." But I've never seen such a nice look as his (Gaily) Me, too, I'm nice today. (To Katherina) Let's profit by it, Miss—and hurry, because I'm getting ready to fly off.

Katherina

(Taking her hand, clumsily) My heart actually told me that the two of us would arrange everything.

Groushenka

I don't want to harm anyone. If I've done it to you, I promise to repair it.

Katherina

(Kissing her hand) Ah, you are generous.

Groushenka

Are you trying to make me confused, dear Miss, by kissing my hand before Alexei Feodorovitch?

Katherina

Make you confused? Me!

Groushenka

Don't be frightened. Before, I was nasty because I was suffering.

Katherina

You've suffered?

Groushenka

That was all five years ago. Everything has been forgotten since he came back.

Katherina

Who came back?

Groushenka

Moussialovitch. It's true. You don't know who Moussialovitch is? He's my inamorata—yes, my first, a Polish officer. I was seventeen when he abandoned me to get married. Ah, what misery! I would have thrown myself in the water, if, at the period the old merchant Samsonov hadn't rescued me.

Katherina

He saved you!

Groushenka

You are very indulgent.

Katherina

He consoled you, protected—

Groushenka

I didn't deceive him, you know—I indeed thought of that. For five years I nourished myself with my love, with my rancor. I hid myself from everyone. I wept whole nights thinking, "Where is he now? No question he is making fun of me with another woman. I will get revenge!" And I wept until sunrise.

Katherina

(Kissing her hand) I understand you. How I understand you.

Groushenka

And then I set myself to amassing money. I've been pitiless, I became strong: Still, I didn't become more reasonable and often, at night between my teeth. I wept, as the little abandoned girl wept five years ago.

Katherina

You still loved the handsome officer, you have never loved anyone but him.

Groushenka

You defend him very excitedly, my dear Miss. You are a bit excited. Perhaps I only loved my rancor. But suddenly, I got some news, a little blessed news! Moussialovitch had become a widow. I hadn't waited vainly, wept, raged for five years. He's come. He wants to see me. "Lord", I thought, "am I going to crawl back to him? Am I going to be such a coward?" And I got mad at myself. It's then that I used Dimitri.

Katherina

You used Dimitri?

Groushenka

From nastiness. To distract me. To keep me from rushing to the other one. (Katherina exchanges a look with Ivan. Groushenka notices it but continues) Old Feodor was pursuing me, also. And I amused myself with both of them. It was necessary to listen to the advice of Samsonov. "If you must choose between the two ", he said to me, "choose the old one on the condition he marry you and give you money. Don't tie yourself to Dimitri, there's nothing to be got from him." It was true. But, money, I laugh at that. I've got it. And Dimitri often pleases me. He's handsome, he's wild, he has a passionate heart. Ah, I'm going to regret him. Moussialovitch is awaiting me at the Mokroie inn.

Katherina

You are leaving this very evening?

Groushenka

Is it time, already? Ah, who can know what's taking place in me! I put on my most beautiful dress to meet you. But Dimitri, if he knew I was leaving. Poor naïve, Mitia. What's going to become of him, once I've left him. And why? Is it because I love this Polish man, Alyosha? Must I pardon him?

Alyosha

You've already pardoned him.

Groushenka

Then I'm going there? If it's not for love it will be for vengeance. I will seduce him, I'll drive him mad—and then I will give him the slip so he can weep in his turn. (She lets herself go on the divan and weeps with her head in the cushions. Katherina sits near her and takes her in her arms)

Katherina

No, little Groushenka. You will forget the harm and you will be happy. There, there—dry your beautiful eyes. There give me back these sweet little hands, these pretty plump hands that I want to kiss because they've brought me joy. No, Groushenka, my bird, we won't listen any more to our fantastic head, we will follow the right path, it's agreed we will be good and generous.

Groushenka

I am bad and not good. I made Dimitri love me to make fun of him—I made him despair.

Katherina

But now you will save him—

Groushenka

Because I will vanish?

Katherina

You will undeceive him, you will make him understand.

Groushenka

So he will love you?

Katherina

(Determined to be patient) Because you love someone else, because all this was only a game?

Groushenka

Oh—dear Miss—that would cause him so much pain! Do you want him to suffer, our Mitia. Do you think me that cruel?

Katherina

But, you promised me.

Groushenka

Ah, no, no. I didn't promise anything. Don't say I promised you.

It's, you, Katherina Ivanovna, who have arranged all this in your head.

Katherina

In that case, I really didn't understand you? You said just now—

Groushenka

What did I say?

Katherina

That you would repair—

Groushenka

Right, right. I really wanted, just now to promise you I didn't know what. But, I remember now, that Dimitri pleases me. The taste one has for men like him doesn't easily wear off. One night, for a whole hour he pleased me. And if he were to please me again? I am so inconstant, so capricious—(Katherina turns away with scorn. Groushenka continues softly) My heart is tender, you know. When I thought just now, what the poor lad has already endured because of me. And if I pity him what is there to do?

Katherina

(No longer able to control herself) Do you expect to humiliate me more?

Groushenka

Ah—now you are no longer going to love me, you who are so nice! I ask your pardon. (She takes Katherina's hand and Katherina, completely disconcerted allows her to hold it) Give your dear little hand. You've kissed mine three times; I'd have to kiss yours 300 times to be even with you. In that case, without promises and conditions? That would make us quite happy so we would release our Dimitri, and you'd be rid of us, right? Dear Miss! What a charming little hand! Well, do you know, my angel, do you know—? I don't want to kiss your hand! (She abruptly releases Katherina's hand and drops it)

Katherina

(Going to Alexei) Alexei—take her away.

Groushenka

Keep this memory, Katherina Ivanovna—you kissed my hand and I didn't kiss yours.

Katherina

Insolent!

Groushenka

Ah, you thought to trap me! It was all arranged. You intended to seduce me with your chocolate. (Busting into laughter) I will tell this adventure to Dimitri. He's really going to laugh.

Katherina

Leave—creature for sale!

Groushenka

For sale? Say there, my little mama, you who play the virgin, didn't you go, all alone, one evening, to the home of a handsome officer to offer your virginity for 4,000 roubles? (Katherina gestures violently toward Groushenka but is restrained by Ivan) In a cabaret, one night, when he was drunk, Dimitri told me about your love.

Alyosha

(Dragging her) Leave, right away.

Groushenka

(To Alyosha) Hush, my pretty boy! I really played my role. She wanted a performance of the great lady and she had it!

And now, I'm leaving for Mokroie! Ah, in an intoxication! Goodbye, everybody. Alioshetchka,—Hello to Dimitri—I won't forget you called me your sister. Tell the lieutenant that Groushenka loved him for only an hour, but let him remember it for his whole life. (She leaves)

Ivan

(To Katherina) Now there's your boarding school imagination, your sentimental pranks. Well, you saw her, that little girl? She defied you. You are jealous.

Katherina

(Head in her hand tearfully) I'm ashamed. (Ivan and Alyosha look at her in silence. A pause) Get out of here, my friends, I'm frightfully ashamed. (They start to go) No, stay. (She gets up) I actually don't know if I love him. (Alyosha gestures to speak) But I've made a decision. Here it is! Here it is! Whatever may happen—even if he marries that creature, I won't abandon him, never! Never! I will follow him with my eyes, I will watch over him—In the end he'll know what I am worth. That's all. And that will be my entire life. (Without looking at Ivan and in a broken voice) My dear Ivan, I hope— that you approve of me—? (Her chin falls on her breast and tears silently run down her face—Ivan turns away)

Alyosha

Katherina Ivanovna—by telling you just now that you must save him—I was mistaken, I didn't know. You suffer too much—It's not possible.

Katherina

(Controlling herself) It's nothing, it's nothing. A little weariness. Nights without sleep. That will pass. With two good friends like you—and your brother, I feel strong.

Ivan

(In a strangled voice) Unfortunately, I am leaving for Moscow this very night.

Katherina

(Overwhelmed but controlling herself) This evening—for Moscow.

Ivan

It's irrevocable.

Katherina

You hadn't told me. This is a bit abrupt.

Ivan

I can't delay any longer.

Katherina

You don't owe me any explanation, my friend. From the moment your decision is made—But when are you thinking of returning?

Ivan

I don't know.

Katherina

Well then, in that case—goodbye. (A silence. Alyosha looks at them without daring to say anything. Katherina is motionless. Ivan slowly goes to her)

Ivan

Goodbye, Katherina. I am leaving you to your difficult duties, to your exercises of conscience. (More bitterly) Wear out your life in the contemplation of your virtues. May you extract from it a glory beautiful enough for you to feel—consoled—in the end—for all the rest.

Katherina

(Stiffening, lips trembling) Good luck, Ivan Feodorovitch. Without you, I hope to reach the goal of my life. For I, too, have a will that doesn't bend. (Ivan starts to leave)

Alyosha

Ivan, don't go. All this is false. You must not leave.

Ivan

There's nothing for me to do here.

Alyosha

Give Katherina the time to get hold of herself.

Ivan

Didn't you hear that she made a decision?

Alyosha

It's only a passing reaction.

Ivan

Her least reactions commit her forever.

Alyosha

Speak to her.

Ivan

I've said all I have to say; I'm leaving forever.

Alyosha

(Desperately to Katherina) Are you going to let him go like this? Ivan, Katherina, I conjure you. Would you actually waste your strength fighting mercilessly? Won't you accept the truth?

Katherina

(Offended) The truth?

Alyosha

Since I've come here, I sought it in your faces. You are struggling against it. It's necessary that someone say it at last! Listen—I know that I'm expressing myself badly. I am not capable of deciding in such a case, and of assigning to each of you your conduct. I know that I am going to wound you. But wouldn't it be better that Dimitri take the hand of Ivan, then yours, and that he join them together? It seems to me,

Katherina that you don't love Dimitri and that the one you love is Ivan.

Katherina

(Furious) You are mad!

Alyosha

You do yourself violence, you torture yourself to love Dimitri. And you make Ivan suffer because you love him.

Ivan

You are mistaken. Katherina has never loved me. She doesn't even cling to my friendship that she implored just now. She had me there, under her hand, you see, to avenge herself on me for the outrages that Dimitri inflicts on her since their first meeting. She never ceases to speak to me of that love!

Katherina

(Tortured, stretching her hands toward Ivan) Ivan!

Ivan

No. I won't take your hand because I don't know how to forgive you at this moment: you've tortured me too conscientiously. Because you love Dimitri! You need him as proof of your spirit of sacrifice, of your moral strength. The more he's humiliated the greater you feel. Each of his crimes is a profit for you. That's the way you love him—or rather, your pride!

Katherina

(Plaintively) Ivan!

Ivan

But you will pass the limits of your strength and his—and that will be my vengeance.

Alyosha

Oh, brother!

Ivan

Not another word! Come (He leaves)

Alyosha

Ah, now he won't come back for anything. It's my fault. I raised his anger. Pardon me: He's been unfair and nasty. Forgive him, Katherina. Forgive my two brothers. They've both got a frenetic and wild instinct in them, from which, may be, the spirit of God is absent.—It's the soul of Karamazov! Don't avenge yourself. Don't undertake anything against them. I'm going to find them, speak to them. I will prevent despair from entering into their heart. Courage, Katherina, courage. God keep you! (He leaves) (Katherina has turned away, motionless. After Alyosha leaves she puts her head in her hands and remains like this for some time. The servant appears. She clears the table, leaves, then comes back with lamps, pulls the curtains and leaves. A ringing. Katherina hears it but doesn't budge. A door opens. A step in the antechamber. Dimitri enters almost running. Katherina stands up. At first he doesn't see her, when he does, steps back lowering his head.)

Dimitri

(Dully) Where is Groushenka?

Katherina

Wretch! This is the ugliest of your crimes. In a cabaret, to this girl, you told everything, all our secrets.

Dimitri

(With deep contrition) I was drunk. The gypsies were singing. But I was crying as I told her—Groushenka was crying, too.

Katherina

You've soiled our memories—of our most beautiful day. Oh, I curse that day.

Dimitri

I curse it, too.

Katherina

Thus you've always scorned me because I went seeking money at your home. You understood nothing, you are incapable of understanding anything noble—I wanted to endure your betrayals. Even this morning, I was determined to forgive you for everything—but not your scorn, not your scorn, that's beyond my strength!

Dimitri

(With wild joy) At last! Be my enemy.

Katherina

Take care. You don't know what I've sacrificed to you.

Dimitri

What have you done with Groushenka?

Katherina

Mitia, choose—there's still time—choose for both of us—good or evil.

Dimitri

I cannot choose. Enough battles. I want to repose in shame. Have pity on me Katia. I'm at the end of my rope. Since this morning I ran to the money-lenders for money. All refused me. But I will return your 3,000 roubles even if I have to go to Siberia. I prefer the chain gang to your love. I will return them to you. And then goodbye, furious woman, goodbye, also, my love! I will ruin myself for not having been able to endure your pride and for no longer loving you. Don't scorn Dimitri—pity him—you see, I kiss your feet. Tell me where Groushenka is—while I am rushing after her, she is escaping. I seek her everywhere. Everyone deceives me. I know she came here. What have you plotted together against me?

Katherina

(Gnashing her teeth) She outraged me, she flouted me.

Dimitri

Ah, ah—the she–devil, the queen of insolence! So much the worse for you. You played the important person! Is she still here? Answer. (Katherina says nothing) Where is she? I beg you in the name of our Lord, tell me where she is. (Silence) She left? (Katherina nods affirmatively) Went to my father's?

She went to the home of the old sinner to get his 3,000 roubles? Yes? She said so? She boasted of it? I know he's waiting for her tonight. (Katherina is obstinately silent. Dimitri in an altered horribly anguished voice) Ah, implacable! But you are not false. Just tell me one thing. Fine, now that you are my enemy, I have faith in you Katherina—I have confidence in you and tell me, do you think Groushenka is capable of going to the old man's place to earn 3,000 roubles?

Katherina

(After a battle with herself, fiercely) I think her capable of anything.

Dimitri

(Leaping) Thanks, I'm going there. (Runs out closing the door behind him)

Katherina

(Suddenly conscious of what she's just done) Dimitri! (she opens the door and rushes outside—she can be heard shouting "Dimitri, Dimitri"—then she comes back in her face overwhelmed testing her hands) He intends to kill! He intends to kill!

CURTAIN

ACT III

The evening of the same day. At the home of Feodor Pavlovitch Karamazov. A large room in white and gold. A mixture of luxury and decay. A small lamp before the icon. To the left a window, further back a door giving on a garden. At back, a door leading to the office. Door to the right under the stair well abutting on a wooden gallery on which rooms open.

AT RISE, the stage is empty. The left door opens abruptly. Dimitri crosses the room and goes out the door at the right. He can be heard shouting at Smerdiakov before they return.

Dimitri

Will you tell me where she's hiding?

Smerdiakov

I swear to you, sir, that Groushenka isn't here. See for yourself.

Dimitri

She came.

Smerdiakov

No.

Dimitri

When will she come?

Smerdiakov

Not before midnight. You've got to get out of here.

Dimitri

Where will he receive her?

Smerdiakov

Here. Feodor Pavlovitch cannot be late. If he finds you—

Dimitri

She'll enter by the gate?

Smerdiakov

Yes.

Dimitri

She'll knock?

Smerdiakov

I already told you that. Mercy, sir, leave!

Dimitri

Two short knocks—followed by three rapid knocks? That's it?

Smerdiakov

That's it, yes. Go out through the kitchen, and leave by the small gate.

Dimitri

(Leaving by the back) Until midnight I'll be on the watch. (Smerdiakov pushes him out. He reappears when Ivan enters. Ivan crosses the room without saying anything. He avoids Smerdiakov and goes up the staircase)

Smerdiakov

My position is frightful, Ivan Feodorovitch. I can no longer see. Your brother is capable of anything . He just came in here like a madman, pushing the furniture, prying in the room, and threatening me with a pistol.

Ivan

Why are you meddling in it?

Smerdiakov

He's the one who's meddling with me. I kept silent, not daring to contradict him—He's made me his confidant.

Ivan

So much the worse for you.

Smerdiakov

Not everyone has your prudence.

Ivan

I forbid you!

Smerdiakov

And from morning to night your father torments me. If Grouchenka doesn't come tonight.

Ivan

She won't come.

Smerdiakov

What! You know it?

Ivan

I know it. Good evening. I won't be here for supper.

Smerdiakov

Well, tomorrow morning it's going to start over "Why didn't she come? When will she come?" Like it was my fault. Ah, you are both going to be exasperated from day to day and make my life so unbearable, that sometimes I think of killing myself to put an end to it.

Ivan

(Disappearing into his room) What do you want me to do about it? (Hardly does Ivan shut his door when Feodor's voice is heard)

Feodor

Smerdiakov (Enters hurriedly) Smerdiakov—he's here. Behind the hedge—I saw his head through the branches—he's lying in wait.

Smerdiakov

Sit down, sir, you are out of breath.

Feodor

(Letting himself go into an armchair) Lock the door. Run find Gregory. Call him. Go! (Smerdiakov leaves. Feodor mops his brow and grouses in his arm chair)

Feodor

(To Gregory) (In a weak voice) Ah—ah—there you are my old Gregory, my good Gregory. Approach.

Gregory

Fear nothing, Master.

Feodor

Give me your hand, my brave Gregory, my well-built Gregory, my body guard. Eh, eh, I'm not afraid when you are here, faithful dog. (Gregory laughs silently) Look at me.

Gregory

Yes, master.

Feodor

How do I look to you, you who are familiar with my face? My eye is not red—the right eye.

Gregory

No, master.

Feodor

Nothing abnormal then?

Gregory

Nothing master.

Feodor

(Reassured, pointing out to Smerdiakov the small packages he held when entering and that he hasn't let go of) You see these are little gifts for my little darling. These are some chocolate, pralines, sugared almonds with liquor. (resuming with anguish to Gregory) Ah, I wasn't good last night, my little daddy. I woke up suddenly. I'm not what I was. My soul trembled in my throat. I was afraid. Because I want to live, you know.

Gregory

You probably ate a bit too much. You need to purge yourself, master. I do that sometimes.

Smerdiakov

Gregory Vassiliev—it is impious to purge oneself. Prayer

suffices a good Christian to cure all ills. Even you think badly. (Feodor tries hard to laugh)

Gregory

You must beat that rogue—master. He respects nothing.

Feodor

Right, yes—By Jove—you understand nothing of fine wit! It's like the other old one, down there, at the monastery "Don't lie", he said. Yuck! We must destroy these monasteries and their mysticism in order to give intelligence to morons. Besides what filth that Russia—or rather its vices. Oh—Russia, too. All this is indecent. I'm going to soak my head in water. Prepare supper, Smerdiakov. As for Dimitri, the no–good—I will have him arrested. It's my right—he threatened me in public—There are laws. (Grumbling he goes upstairs and enters his room)

Gregory

What happened this morning at the monastery?

Smerdiakov

Yuck! Antics—scandals.

Gregory

So, the holy old man didn't reconcile them!

Smerdiakov

Feodor would not give in. Dimitri will not be stopped by anything. It smells of crime here, Gregory Vassiliev. Ivan's just waiting for that. He is laughing at them and regales himself at their expense. That one isn't stupid. (As he speaks he pulls a little dressing box from his pocket and passes a comb through his hair)

Gregory

(Crossing himself) Shut up, vermin!

Smerdiakov

(Between his teeth) He treats me like a lackey. I know him better than he knows me.

Gregory

Because you apprenticed in Moscow, you take yourself for someone. You play the gentleman with your pomade and your white linen. A coward! That's what you are!

Smerdiakov

(Arranging the table) I would have been a different man if I had been raised differently.

Gregory

Raised differently—the son of a slut!

Smerdiakov

(Shaking) You told everybody, right? I know quite well I'm the son of a slut—they threw it enough in my face in Moscow! And here, in the market, they say out loud, in front of me, that my mother was only four feet high and that her hair was always coagulated with mud.

Gregory

That pains you?

Smerdiakov

That doesn't pain me—it shames me. I know indeed that I am a Smerdiakov. All my childhood they beat me.

Gregory

You only took pleasure in hanging cats to bury them with great ceremony.

Smerdiakov

You, Gregory Vassiliev—you used to cuff me.

Gregory

You disputed the Evangelist!

Smerdiakov

I raised reasonable objections that you were incapable of replying to. It's as a consequence of these corrections that I had my first epileptic crisis—I know indeed that I am only an epileptic, a dish washer. (He plays with a knife that he jams in the table. Suddenly utters a deep sigh) Ah, if I had a certain sum in my pocket.

Gregory

What would you do?

Smerdiakov

I would have cleared out a long time ago.

Gregory

And then—

Smerdiakov

I would open a café-restaurant in Moscow—and no one would be capable of making a cuisine like mine.

Feodor

(From his room) Is supper ready?

Smerdiakov

Get out. The master only wants to be served by me. (He goes out)

Feodor

(Coming downstairs) You are still here whining, old man? We will beat this Smerdiakov, I promise you. (Gregory leaves grumbling. Smerdiakov returns bearing a pâté)

Feodor

(Going to the table) Oh—oh—a fish pâté! Now that completes my joy and doubles my appetite. For you are a veritable artist, Smerdiakov, with the fish pâté! Well, and the other one—Ivan? Is he coming down?

Smerdiakov

No—he's not coming down.

Feodor

So much the better. Go and look through the keyhole—and see what he's doing in his room. (Smerdiakov quietly climbs the stairs and peers through the keyhole) Eh?

Smerdiakov

(Coming down) Nothing, he's seated at a chair staring in front of him.

Feodor

He's meditating, he's calculating—he's fretting because nothing is arranged to suit him. Will he go to the Tchermachnia?

Smerdiakov

I don't know.

Feodor

I'm dying of hunger. Uncover. (Admiring the pâté) How golden it is! How juicy! (Begins to eat) It's fine: at midnight, according to her letter—my Groushenka, right? Yes—something to drink. You are looking at me? I am seedy, right? Bah, with my arched nose, and my double chin—I resemble an old Roman of the decadence. And then, I purchased a new silk handkerchief. I will open it myself. She will come in like this—a bit confused "Here I am Feodor Pavlovitch—were you expecting me?" Yes, I'm expecting her. I'm as amorous as a cat!

Smerdiakov

By the way, sir—the 3,000 roubles? Where is the envelope with 3,000 roubles?

Feodor

Under my mattress.

Smerdiakov

Bad hiding place.

Feodor

You think so? Clamber up and bring me the package. (Smerdiakov obeys. Feodor points to Ivan's door) Hush! Quietly. (Smerdiakov comes back and gives the envelope to Feodor) There. And now where? In this armchair?

Smerdiakov

Why not behind the icon?

Feodor

Bravo. Ah, indeed, for goodness sake. That's admirable. Behind the icon. Ah, ah—yes, Dimitri is never going to look for them there. And Grushenka is really going to laugh when I pull this little gift for her from behind the icon. Now there—dim the lamps. We'll relight them tonight. It's to see clearly that I burn oil—and not to honor the girls.—ha, ha, ha—(He drinks and strangles noisily)

Smerdiakov

What's wrong sir—you will make yourself ill.

Feodor

(In the midst of hiccups) Nothing—swallowed wrong—so funny—ah, ah, ah—behind the icon. (Laughing to croak. He laughs so long that Ivan, attracted by the noise appears. Feodor, speechless, stops laughing) What—what is it you want, huh?

Ivan

Nothing. I heard you laugh. That's all.

Feodor

You want supper?

Ivan

I'm not hungry, thanks—But I will keep you company if that doesn't displease you.

Feodor

(Between his teeth) As you like. (Ivan sits opposite Feodor—who becomes mute, stuffing himself) You don't say anything.

Ivan

I'm admiring you appetite.

Feodor

Smerdiakov. I'm done. (To Ivan as Smerdiakov clears the table) Do you think Alyosha will be vexed? I regret having been lacking a bit in manners—this morning, before your monk.

Ivan

Truly?

Feodor

You don't believe me? I see that from your manner. You take me for a buffoon—Heavens, here's Balaam's ass coming loaded with liquors. (Smerdiakov places viols and glasses, then withdraws a bit, seeming absorbed.) You'll actually have a glass of my old cognac? I know that you love it. You are not, one of those sots, who drink water. To love cognac you must have wit. And we are people of wit, aren't we, Ivan? And all our life we will continue to warm our back, to fill our belly and drink cognac. It's God himself who must have arranged all that.

Ivan

By Jove.

Feodor

(Leaning on elbows) Ivan—all this tortures me, all this cognac. Don't mock a weak old man—you don't love me and you have no reason to love me. But look, tell me—just between us, Ivan. Does God exist—yes or no? (Ivan empties his glass without replying) I need to know, my son.

Ivan

(Leaning forward on his elbows and staring in his father's face) No—God does not exist.

Feodor

Really true? Alyosha insists that he exists. (Noticing Smerdiakov who, motionless has not lost a word of the conversation) Are you going to beat it, Jesuit? (Smerdiakov moves away but doesn't leave) He'll stay there, listening to us. It's probably you who interest him. What have you done to him?

Ivan

Nothing. It's an air he gives himself.

Feodor

And then—immortality? Does it exist?

Ivan

No.

Feodor

(With a dull lightness which he controls) You are sure of it, my little Ivan? You are not making fun of me? You wouldn't deceive a poor man who no longer has a long time to live, eh? No immortality, not the least little bit of immortality?

Ivan

Nothing.

Feodor

Meaning—an absolute zero, or a small fraction of unity. Not even a fraction of a fraction?

Ivan

Absolute zero.

Feodor

(No longer able to control himself) Why in that case—why—in that case, Ivan—

Everything is permitted?

Ivan

Yes, everything is permitted, father.

Feodor

Hush! Don't say that. Let's keep that between ourselves, my child. To your health (They drink) Dear Ivan, I'm pleased to see you seated there, opposite me—and that we are drinking together like two friends.

Ivan

Yes.

Feodor

(A foot on the table) We could be so happy on earth.

Ivan

(With effort) Yes.

Feodor

I am still a man, you know, my colleague, and I intend to continue to be one for twenty years more. Only, I'm aging, I'm becoming more and more repulsive, and they don't want to come to my place as willingly, the little pussycats. In that case, I will need all my kopecks.

Ivan

Naturally.

Feodor

(Completely drunk) That's what I want you to know, my dear son Ivan, that I've amassed and continue to amass for myself alone, I intend to live in my mud and as long as possible. One is very comfortable in the mud. As for me, I don't want to go to paradise with Alyosha—assuming it exists, it's not the place for a man of wit. (Puts his hand on the bottle)

Ivan

You've had enough to drink.

Feodor

Psst! Leave it there. Yet another little glass, only one. I won't croak because of a little glass. (He tenders his glass that Ivan fills) Do you know that story of Van Zohn who was murdered at the girls' place?

Ivan

I don't care to know it.

Feodor

Fine. In that case I'm going to tell you the strange adventure of Elizabeth Smerdiatchaia, the slut. Imagine that she ran the roads without any other dress than a simple slip—and which didn't lack a certain—even though she was dirty—you see, my little piggy, in my life I've never found a woman ugly. Each has her charm: that's my rule. And the fact alone of sex is already enormous. When you go to Tchermachnia. I will point out a girl to you. She goes barefoot, but—so then, one summer night, I returned from dinner with some jolly companions, and there, against a hedge, sleeping in the nettles and completely asleep, we noticed Elizabeth Smerdiat—(Blindly intoxicated Feodor hasn't spoken guardedly. Smerdiakov has cocked an ear and tiptoed toward the table. Ivan observes the lackey. Following his look Feodor turns slowly with fright, and seeing Smerdiakov leaning towards him, foam on his lips, limbs agitated by a trembling epilepsy—He stops abruptly. An idiotic smile wanders over his face. Ivan looks at the ceiling while rocking in his chair. Silence)

Smerdiakov

(Whose hateful expression degenerates into a plaintive sneer) It's eleven o'clock, sir—

Feodor

Well—why—my lad—yes. (Smerdiakov leaves slowly)

Feodor

(Furious, to Ivan) Why didn't you stop me?

Ivan

I wanted to see how far you would go.

Feodor

From nastiness? You come to scorn me in my own house—

Ivan

I'm leaving. It's the cognac talking.

Feodor

You didn't fail to pour it for me. Take it away, immediately—your evil eyes watch me; they spy on me—you have an ulterior motive. Say what it is! (Ivan raises his shoulders with scorn) Yes, you shut up, as always. You only know how to shut up and make fun of others in silence. That's how you give yourself the airs of a savant. Or, if you speak—you make grimaces—you have no right to judge me! You are not better than I am, my comrade. (One can feel an inexpressible disgust rising in Ivan. Alyosha appears)

Feodor

(To Alyosha) Why did you come? I didn't invite anyone.

Alyosha

(Going to him) How irritable you are, father.

Feodor

(Aside, low) My dear only son! Be my good angel—get him out of here. He scares me more than the other one.

Alyosha

He's hurting. Manage him.

Feodor

(Turning on his heels) Pfft—Smerdiakov—come dress me (Goes upstairs followed by Smerdiakov, then somewhat softened to Ivan) I beg you, Ivan, leave tonight for Tchermachnia—I entreat you. (Ivan striding about, shakes his head negatively) No? You refuse? You want to mount guard here? You want to know how much I will give to Groushenka when she comes to see me? And you are pushing Dimitri to flee with her so as to possess Katherina Ivanovna who is rich—Those are your thoughts and your calculations, good-for-nothing! Well! know that I will marry Groushenka this very moment—if it suits me. As for Katherina—you shan't have her, you hear—you shan't have her—I forbid you to. (He goes into his room followed by Smerdiakov. Alyosha watches Ivan who continues stride back and forth in silence. Then he lowers his eyes as if ashamed and afraid. As he starts to speak Ivan gestures for him to be silent)

Ivan

(As if to himself) I remained an hour too long. I ought not to have come back here—in this stench, to see this old man. I shouldn't have done it. Hate is going to spoil the pleasure of leaving.

Alyosha

So you are leaving?

Ivan

In an hour I'll be far from here.

Alyosha

What are you going to do, Ivan?

Ivan

Live for myself and let everyone go to the devil! To live as a man of wit as my father says. (Stopping and rapping his fist on the table) I f you knew what I've endured here! He winked at me, and clapped me on the shoulder. He's fifty-seven and I'm twenty-three. Is that all the difference there is between us? To be supported like this on his luxury is ignoble. Ah, Lyosha by thirty I'll have given up drinking from disgust. But until thirty, what to harken to, if not desires?—at least to be a strong man, like you, who knows his goal, and knows how to adhere to the right. I prefer strong men. And you, Lyosha, do you love me?

Alyosha

Yes, I love you. There's one thing that I understood in you—it's that you are as naively young as the other young people of twenty-three.

Ivan

Yes.

Alyosha

A completely fresh young man.

Ivan

Yes, Alyosha. To become a man is frightful. I don't want to ripen. I want to remain an adolescent like you.—And one who feels virtuous to such a degree that he thinks himself incapable of being satisfied. Leaving her place, before, I said to myself my youth will conquer all obstacles, when all the horrors of disillusion, of treachery shall come to strike me, I will want to live. To extinguish in myself the passion to live, there is no despair strong enough.

Alyosha

What despair are you speaking of?

Ivan

Don't try to find out. I am detached from everything. I swear to you. Ah, I didn't think it would be so easy. In a minute I wiped out six months of my life. At our age one is rich. And anything is better than to endure an insult.

Alyosha

In that case you don't love Katherina.

Ivan

Possibly. You see, nothing has been able to tyrannize over me. I am excitable. I don't have the time to wait and torment myself. So much the worse! I'm starting over—

Alyosha

Katherina loves you.

Ivan

That's as may be.

Alyosha

Why did you tell her that she never loved you?

Ivan

I did it purposely.

Alyosha

Why make her suffer?

Ivan

Let her suffer!

Alyosha

Brother, have you considered that maddened by sorrow Katherina might avenge herself on Dimitri?

Ivan

Am I my brother's keeper?

Alyosha

That's the response of—(Smerdiakov, carrying Feodor's clothes and slippers to the office, crosses the stage and leaves. The two brothers hold their peace until he's passed)

Ivan

The response of Cain, right? But can I spend my life watching over these fools? I no longer want to look behind me. I intend to act only at my whim, and depend on no one. I've broken away, I've left—Do you understand? I can do no matter what.

Alyosha

(Sadly) Ah, yes—All desires are permitted, right?

Ivan

So be it! I won't gainsay myself: everything is permitted. Alyosha, I am fine. I intend to celebrate my liberty, drink to my liberty.

Alyosha

No brother, let's not drink—I am so sad. (a silence) Father Zossima is dead.

Ivan

(With a strange smile) Now here's what you give to us, little Karamazov.

Alyosha

He's sending me into the world.

Ivan

And it's toward me that you are coming first.

Alyosha

He commanded me.

Ivan

With your beautiful gray eyes. Which for the last three months, question me. You want to know me. I've seen you watching me so attentively. I, too, my dear, before leaving forever, I would like to make your acquaintance . It's much too late. Why didn't you make a sign, speak the first word?

Alyosha

Why didn't I dare? Perhaps all this wouldn't have happened.

Ivan

Nothing has happened, Lyosha. Some thoughts bad dreams, at most.

Alyosha

You still want to escape! I will no longer leave your secret at rest, Vania. With what are you discontent? Say it, say it. Is there nothing about which I can soothe you, brother? What are you suffering from? I would like to take on your suffering.

Ivan

(Shrugging his shoulders)Novice! I would show you my suffering except that you cannot grasp it yet. And grasping it, what could you do about it? One cannot love, despite all the love one has in oneself, one cannot. It's a physical impossibility, an impossibility. As for understanding the suffering of others—

Alyosha

Whatever may be your suffering, Ivan—I know it cannot corrupt you. If something remains visible in you it's the nobility of your soul.

Ivan

Forever filled with torment, in distress in battle, and yet so new! Don't ask me to explain. All the reasons I've understood, only serve to mask in me a horrible instinct. All reasons are cowards. I want no more of them. Let me live! That suffices for me. The blue sky, the spring and its fresh flowers content me. We have life before us. It will end well by carrying us somewhere, where we will land. You understand?

Alyosha

(Lowering his eyes) Yes.

Ivan

Distance yourself—go—I'm no longer a man who is good to question. Already, I can no longer reveal all my thoughts.

Alyosha

Brother, I'm not afraid. Don't think that I fear the mind that's in you, even if it is rebellious.

Ivan

No revolt! One cannot live in rebellion! And I'm going to live despite everything. No rebellion—oh, no. But despair, or rather—indignation, yes, a refusal! There it is: I do not accept the world.

Alyosha

(Gently) For all that, you love it, Vania.

Ivan

I'm unable to curse love.

Alyosha

The blue heavens, spring—and its new flowers—

Ivan

Until I'm thirty—

Alyosha

But until you are thirty—how are you going to live with such hell in your heart and your head?

Ivan

Now that's my grief, that's my rancor against God—that he put all this fervor into us, this intrepidity which casts me into life and which opposes me to it, who has inflicted me with this thirst to live, this invincible impatience—stronger, more invincible than my disgust. No, no—no rebellion, but an evil ferocity. I don't wish to live according to the principles of my nature and I see—only rage in my heart—Vengeance is necessary for me.

Alyosha

I wish you it, Ivan, I wish you it soon and that it consume you like grain in the earth, it dies and is defeated, and destroyed so long as it bears all its fruits. You were right brother, I am too weak, alas! To assuage your ills. God will relieve you of them. (Ivan lowers his head a bit. Smerdiakov slowly crosses the stage)

Ivan

(To Smerdiakov with sudden fury) Will you stop spying? (To Alyosha) He still had his ear at the door. (Pushing Smerdiakov) Get out of here (To Alyosha) He follows me everywhere like a shadow.

Alyosha

Calm down.

Ivan

I cannot endure his abject familiarity. What have I to do with him? Ah, that such a good–for–nothing can disturb me to this degree! I've got a headache, Lyosha. I'm chagrined. I intended to be so happy this evening. I'm chagrined. That weighs on me. I was hoping, in leaving, to leave at least one friend. And see what a bitter memory you will keep of this final meeting. Don't take me for a no-good (Alyosha rises, leans over his brother and hugs him)

Alyosha

Ivan, you recall our childhood.

Ivan

I remember everything Alyosha, and now we must separate.

Alyosha

And the others? And Katherina? What's going to become of them?

Ivan

Do like me—don't think about it.

Alyosha

What's wrong with you? You seem to be breathing with difficulty?

Ivan

It will pass off soon—in the fresh air.

Alyosha

(Hanging his head) You imagine you can rid yourself of your thoughts.

Ivan

I'm going to light you out, little brother. (Taking a lamp and leading Alyosha to the door)

Alyosha

How hard your face is—and how much I love it.

Ivan

Let's embrace again one time. Then, goodbye. (They separate. Alyosha leaves) (Smerdiakov has gone to sit on a step of the staircase, as if overwhelmed, head in his hands. After leaving Alyosha, Ivan starts toward his room and finds Smerdiakov blocking his way in the shadow. He stops, expecting the lackey to get out of his way. Smerdiakov smiles vaguely.)

Ivan

Let me pass! (Without rising Smerdiakov recoils so Ivan can pass but rubs against him. Ivan goes up two steps then turns toward Smerdiakov who continues to watch him)

Smerdiakov

(Turning away, low) You astonish me, sir.

Ivan

(Frowning) What is it that astonishes you?

Smerdiakov

Why aren't you going to Tchermachnia?

Ivan

You are going to question me, too?

Smerdiakov

Feodor Pavlovitch himself entreated you—

Ivan

The devil take you! Speak more clearly.

Smerdiakov

Oh—it's nothing very important—rather it was just to say something. (He shuts up, sighs and begins to tremble)

Ivan

(About to enter his room) How your teeth chatter.

Smerdiakov

(Shivering greatly) I am sure, sir, that I will soon have, perhaps tonight, a long—a very long epileptic crisis.

Ivan

(Coming to him) What do you mean, very long?

Smerdiakov

Yes—it will last more or less a long while—several hours or a day or two.

Ivan

How can you foresee that you will have a crisis—tonight? When you had your great crisis you fell in the loft.

Smerdiakov

I go there, each day to the loft—and if I don't fall in the loft I will fall in the wine cellar where you know service obliges me to go all the time...

Ivan

(Going close to him) Do I understand you? You are proposing to feign tonight an attack of epilepsy and to make it last for three days? Right? You smile.

Smerdiakov

Let's admit that I can feign an attack. Don't I have the right to safeguard my life that is threatened? If Groushenka comes to Feodor Pavlovitch's, your brother won't be able to hold a sick man responsible for being unable to prevent it.

Ivan

And why speak to me like this?

Smerdiakov

To have your advice, Ivan Feodorovitch.

Ivan

I told you that Groushenka won't come.

Smerdiakov

But if it happens that Dimitri Feodorovitch commits some stupidity on his father, I don't want to be taken as his accomplice.

Ivan

Why would you be taken as his accomplice?

Smerdiakov

Because of signals.

Ivan

What signals?

Smerdiakov

Since you are interested in the situation I will confess to you, sir, that in the event she were to decide on a nocturnal visit, Groushenka must rap on the window here—First two spaced raps—then three hurried ones. Feodor Pavlovitch thinks we alone know of the signals, himself, Groushenka and me. But you see your brother knows them.

Ivan

How dared you inform him of them?

Smerdiakov

From terror to convince him of my fidelity.

Ivan

If you see him use them, don't let him do it.

Smerdiakov

And if I have my crisis?

Ivan

Warn Gregory. Let him watch.

Smerdiakov

For the last three days he's been sleeping in the small common pavilion. If Dimitri jumps the fence or goes through the hedge, he can get to the house without Gregory hearing him.

Ivan

Then why do you advise me to go to Tchermachnia?—I intend to know what you are thinking.

Smerdiakov

(Out of breath) What do my thoughts matter here?

Feodor

(Calling from his room) Smerdiakov.

Smerdiakov

(Pulling Ivan and speaking in an urgent voice) I am speaking from interest for you. You know quite well that I am entirely devoted. In your place I wouldn't run the risk of being mixed up in such a scandal. You understand things too well not to understand that, Ivan Feodorovitch. (Ivan is unable to prevent himself from listening to the end. He's agitated by a kind laughter he cannot release. He climbs the stairs, then on the first landing leans over the balustrade.)

Ivan

If you want to know, I'm leaving for Moscow in an hour.

Smerdiakov

(Weakly) That's the best thing you could do.

Feodor

(Calling from his room) Smerdiakov.

Ivan

(Pulling his trunk from his room) Help me.

Smerdiakov

Sir, your father's calling me.

Ivan

(Placing the trunk on Smerdiakov's shoulders) Come on! Place it in the garden. I will see about the coachman. (Smerdiakov obeys. Ivan goes back into his room for his coat. At the foot of the stairs he seems to hesitate for a moment)

Smerdiakov

(Returning) Aren't you going to take leave of your father?

Ivan

The train for Moscow leaves at 12:50. The station is a long way away. I barely have time to catch it. (Cocking his ear) It's him I hear walking upstairs?

Smerdiakov

Yes. You have nothing more to tell me, sir?

Ivan

And you?

Smerdiakov

I've spoken more than you.

Ivan

You didn't think, did you, that I will leave?

Smerdiakov

It's true to say it is always good to chat with a man of wit. Shall I accompany you, sir?

Ivan

Leave me alone. (He pushes Smerdiakov back and shuts the door. Smerdiakov leaves against the door to listen. Feodor can be heard calling. Smerdiakov blows out the light and leaves furtively, shutting the door behind him) (Feodor emerges from his room with a lit candle in his hand, dressed in a robe with a red scarf and lace frills.)

Feodor

Smerdiakov! (Looking at his watch) Eh, eh—quarter to midnight! You are there my little Smerdiakov? (He comes down the stairs. His motions become increasingly feverish, visibly uneasy he goes from door to door, calling, swearing.

Finally, he goes up to Ivan's room, opens it—and comes down the stairs) Gone! Gone! Are they going to leave me? (He starts looking around again when at the window on the left he hears the signal, two raps—then three quick raps. He stops, places the candle down and goes to the window. Emotion strangles his voice) Groushenka, is that you? (The raps are repeated. He gently opens the window and leans out to look outside) Is that you? Come closer. Where are you, my little darling, my little angel? (Silence. Smerdiakov reenters on tip-toe hiding behind the furniture. He watches Feodor, waits tortured by impatience. Feodor continues to talk out the window.) Groushenka—Why don't you want to answer me? I am alone. Ah-she–devil. I will know how to hunt you out. (Feodor goes out. Then Smerdiakov who was kneeling behind an armchair goes to hide behind the pillar from which the icon hangs)

CURTAIN

ACT IV

At Mokroie. The second floor of the inn. A huge cabinet whose walls are hung with faded blue paper. An alcove whose half drawn curtains allow a low bed to be seen. At the rear a huge bay window opening on a balcony which dominates the court of the inn. To the right, near the audience against the wall—a divan beneath a large mirror—a table in front of the divan—an armchair near the table.

Moussialovitch is half stretched on the divan smoking his pipe from which he draws thick whiffs. Vroubelski—on the other side of the table plays patience. Groushenka is seated near Moussialovitch, with an absent attitude. The table is lit by two torches. The heavy silence of boredom.

Groushenka

(Pulling away from Moussialovitch who leans toward her) Couldn't you leave your pipe?

Moussialovitch

(Putting his pipe down) I was admiring—

Groushenka

I am beautiful, right? It's in your honor.

Moussialovitch

This jewel is worth not less than 1000 roubles.

Groushenka

You know it. (Silence) (Groushenka sighs. She gets up and crosses the room. From a distance she watches Moussialovitch with disgust as he pours a drink and whispers something in the ear of Vroubelski which causes Vroubelski to nod in approval)

Groushenka

(Low) Five years of my life.

Moussialovitch

What are you saying, my pretty?

Groushenka

I said—five years (Gets up)

Moussialovitch

(Going to her) Do you know, my darling, that in five years you have embellished in a way that—

Groushenka

I am no longer that little skinny thing. We've both changed. You were so caressing, so gay—

Moussialovitch

(Gallantly) Why—

Groushenka

(Stopping him, hand extended) You haven't said anything to me of my rings. Are they to your taste?

Moussialovitch

Magnificent (He kisses her hand)

Groushenka

(Barely controlling herself) Feel the material of my dress—See what I'm worth.

Moussialovitch

I don't understand.

Groushenka

(Sitting down) In the past, you sang me songs which seemed so pretty to me. Don't you know any anymore?

Moussialovitch

Oh—songs. My word, no.

Groushenka

So much the worse. I would have loved, like before. (She hums and soon stops to furtively dry her eyes)

Moussialovitch

You are sad? (Leaning) My beloved—

Groushenka

Don't call me your beloved.

Moussialovitch

(Stung) Must I call you "my sister"

Groushenka

Someone good, someone pure called me "my sister" today. I blushed. Why that knocked over my heart. For the first time someone had pity on me, they pardoned me, they loved me despite my shame, and for something besides my shame. And I felt like tearing off this jewelry of giving up all the money I have and then making myself a serving girl.

Moussialovitch

Look, look Groushenka what are all these mental wanderings? You are a bit tired, no question. You need rest. Come. I'm going to take you there. (Takes her by the arm)

Groushenka

(Getting away) Leave me alone. It is late. More than one in the morning. I am going to leave.

Moussialovitch

(With a glance at Vroubelski who contemplates the scene) Leave? You can't be thinking of leaving at this hour?

Groushenka

(Taking her cloak) This very moment.

Moussialovitch

The innkeeper must be sleeping.

Groushenka

(Dressing) I'll wake him.

Moussialovitch

Then why did you come?

Groushenka

To see you. I've seen you, goodbye.

Moussialovitch

Ah, that's the way it is! You rushed at my call.

Groushenka

At your call, yes, like a dog. You whistled—I crawled. A cowardly heart like mine.

Moussialovitch, someone loves me. I made him despair for you.

Moussialovitch

(Ready to be annoyed) I am not asking you for confidences. (The noise of carriage bells can be heard in the court yard)

Groushenka

A carriage! I'm lucky. Quick. (She starts to leave)

Moussialovitch

(Blocking her) But—but—my little one—I won't allow you to leave like this.

Groushenka

You won't let me leave?

Moussialovitch

No.

Groushenka

You aren't going to keep me by force?

Moussialovitch

If it's money you want, I'll give you some.

Groushenka

Release me or I'll scream

Moussialovitch

Hush. (Voices can be heard outside. Through the glass the innkeeper Trifon Boristisch, can be seen lantern in hand. He indicates to Dimitri who follows him, where the Poles are.)

Vroubelski

What's this uproar?

Moussialovitch

I don't know. Maybe we can go into the next room. (He starts pulling Groushenka when Dimitri appears. Groushenka, seeing Dimitri lets out a piercing scream)

Dimitri

I'm leaving—fear nothing.

Moussialovitch

What's all this?

Groushenka

(In a breathe) It's you.

Dimitri

For a moment—near you—only to see you. (Strides toward the table behind which the Poles have barricaded themselves) I am a traveler, gentleman. Passing through—would you indeed permit a traveler to remain with you until morning—for the last time?

Moussialovitch

Sir, we are here in a hotel, and there are other cabinets.

Dimitri

I am going to explain everything to you sir. I came at a full gallop for an hour of my last day, in this room—and then, I will rid you of me. That's sworn.

Moussialovitch

(To Groushenka) You know this gentleman?

Groushenka

Lieutenant Dimitri Feodorovitch Karamazov. (Presenting) Lieutenant Moussialovitch

Dimitri

(Seizing Moussialovitch's hand) Ah! Lieutenant. (Bowing to Vroubelski) Sir!?

Vroubelski

Vroubelski

Dimitri

Mr. Vroubelski. Enchanted!

Groushenka

Come on—you are making me laugh. Sit down, Dimitri, and stop talking.

Moussialovitch

Since my queen desires it.

Dimitri

Sir, I am grateful to you. (The coachman Andre followed by Trifon Boristisch enter bearing voluminous packages)

Dimitri

(To Coachman) Place that here. Some good stuff. Heavens, Andre—fifteen roubles for your trip and five for your tip because you got me here very nicely. And remember Mr. Karamazov who thanks you for your kindness.

Andre

Sir, you scare me. I will be content with 5 roubles.

Dimitri

(Throwing money at him) May the devil take you!

Andre

(Low, going to Trifon) Trifon Boristisch—you are witness.

Dimitri

(Returning to Moussialovitch) Take back up your pipe, sir. I don't wish to disturb anyone. This imbecile of a Mitia will no longer disturb anyone. It's all over. Gentlemen behold in me a poor man, a beggar. I've lost everything. I had everything—I no longer have anything. (So saying he pulls from his pocket a bunch of bank notes that he places beside him on the table)

Vroubelski

(Putting his finger on a package of roubles) You call this nothing. At least 3,000 roubles.

Dimitri

(Quickly pocketing his money) I wasn't speaking of money. To the devil with money. I was speaking of women. (He pulls out a pistol that he starts to load)

Moussialovitch

You are loading a pistol now?

Dimitri

My God, yes. I'm loading a pistol.

Moussialovitch

And you are examining the bullet?

Dimitri

It interests me.

Moussialovitch

You say—

Dimitri

(Putting the pistol in his pocket) Absurdities, my dear Moussialovitch. All merely absurdities. (Suddenly to Vroubelski) You, sir, do you know how to withdraw?

Vroubelski

(Speechless) How's that?

Dimitri

To withdraw, disappear, leave the way free to the being that you cherish—and to the one that you hate—and say to them "May God be with you—pass—and as for me, enough!" (He seizes the back of the chair with both hands and bursts out into sobbing)

Groushenka

That's the way he is?—Why are you crying? It's shameful. If there was only something wrong.

Dimitri

I—I am not crying—See my joy.

Groushenka

That's the way—be gay. I am happy that you came, very happy, you hear, Mitia? I want him to stay with us—and if he goes, I'll go with him—That's all—

Moussialovitch

Whatever Groushenka wants is law. Sir, be welcome among us.

Dimitri

Let's drink as friends. Hey! Trifon, champagne!

Groushenka

You did well to bring some champagne. But what you brought better was yourself. It's boring here! You came to have a party, right?

Moussialovitch

(To Vroubelski) What time is it? (Vroubelski gestures that he doesn't know)

Dimitri

You don't have a watch. Twenty past two.

Moussialovitch

Too late to have a party.

Groushenka

Go to sleep Polish gentlemen, but let others amuse themselves.

Dimitri

(To Trifon who brings champagne) Did you unpack the luggage? There's some foie de gras, smoked fish, caviar. Listen shall we have gypsies?

Trifon

No gypsies here. The authorities chased them out. But Jewish musicians remain to us. Would you like for them to be sent for?

Dimitri

Have them sent for! Have them sent for! Wake everybody up! Men, women. Like the first time. They'll remember, I think? There will be 200 roubles for the chorus. (Offering him money) Here, take that.

Moussialovitch

You treat bank notes like excrement, my word.

Trifon

For that price the whole village will rise up. But are you going to spend so much money for sluts and to smoke cigars before these rustics who stink? I'm going to kick my own girls out of bed, and with kicks in the ass even! They will sing for you. (He leaves)

Dimitri

(Accompanying him) Hurrah! I want a riot, a thunder clap, a wedding which will be remembered for a long time. (Slapping his pocket) There's plenty of money.

Groushenka

(Who's never stopped watching him, passes behind him and says low) Your sleeve.

Dimitri

Huh?

Groushenka

(Whispering) Pull up your sleeve.

Dimitri

(Looking at the cuff of his shirt and hiding it under his sleeve)

Good. (Going back to the table) You aren't drinking, gentlemen? (To Vroubelski who rapidly strides around) Sir—what's your name?

Vroubelski

Vroubelski.

Dimitri

What's the matter with you that you are walking about like that, Mr. Vroubelski? Take your glass. To Russia, gentlemen, and let's be brothers! (They drink and replace their glasses) Now, what are we going to do while waiting for the girls? (Noticing cards on the table) Hey, by Jove, a bank!

Moussialovitch

I am at your service, sir.

Dimitri

Well, begin. Take the bank, hold the cards. I want you to win lots of money, sir.

Vroubelski

To your places.

Dimitri

What have you got in the bank?

Moussialovitch

Whatever you like—one hundred, two hundred roubles.

Dimitri

Come on—ten roubles on Jacks.

Vroubelski

(Smiling at Groushenka) And as for me, I place a rouble on the Queen of hearts—(They play)

Dimitri

Parole!

Vroubelski

I place yet another rouble.

Dimitri

Lost. Another on seven. Lost again.

Groushenka

(Low to Dimitri) Enough!

Dimitri

On the seven! On the seven!

Moussialovitch

You've lost 200 roubles. Do you want to double again?

Dimitri

What? I've already lost 200 roubles? So much the worse—I

double!

Groushenka

(Placing two hands on the cards) That's enough of this!

Dimitri

Why?

Groushenka

Because. I don't like it, you won't play anymore. Spit, rather.

Moussialovitch

You're joking, my darling?

Groushenka

Ah! You shut up. What shame! Lord—What's become of him?

Dimitri

(Looking at Groushenka) Did he?

Groushenka

Twice I saw him switch the card.

Moussialovitch

Madame, I am a gentleman.

Groushenka

And as for me I wept for five years. A thief.

Vroubelski

I won't allow—

Groushenka

The other one, too—Shake his sleeve.

Vroubelski

(Beating a retreat) Dirty slut. (Dimitri leaps on him and goes to throw him into the stairway)

Groushenka

(Clapping her hands) Like a package! Like a package!

Moussialovitch

I came to be pardoned for marrying, but I find a person with so much effrontery—

Groushenka

Go back where you came from!

Dimitri

(Reentering) I deposited him a bit hard. (He laughs) (To Moussialovitch) I beg you, sir—(Points to the door)

Moussialovitch

Truly, your lovers surprise me.

Dimitri

I've never been her lover.

Groushenka

Let him go.

Dimitri

Get out of here.

Trifon

(Running at the uproar) My little father, you won't take back the money he stole from you?

Dimitri

Let him keep it for his consolation.

Groushenka

Bravo, Mitia! Good boy!

Trifon

The musicians are here, sir, they're going to come up. (He leaves)

Dimitri

(Closing the door and turning to Groushenka—wild and gay)
Groushenka at last! I find you again, naughty one.

Groushenka

(Opening her arms to him) You saved me!

Dimitri

(Low, twisting her hands) Oh!

Groushenka

If you knew how you frightened me when you came in! How did you find me? Who told you?

Dimitri

Your maid. She explained everything to me.

Groushenka

Fenia? You went to my place?

Dimitri

Twice. The first time Fenia didn't want to tell me anything—She was afraid. Ah, if she had spoken right away—This wouldn't have happened. It was only after—when it was too late. I wept, looking for you, I wept like a little child.

Groushenka

Where'd you look for me?

Dimitri

Everywhere.

Groushenka

Yes, I left you behind me, on my trail.

Dimitri

I ran to Katherina Ivanovna's. You'd left. Then, no more doubt. Smerdiakov told me that my father was waiting for you.

Groushenka

You thought to find me at Feodor Pavlovitch's?

Dimitri

Forgive me. Yes—I watched the door for an hour.

Groushenka

And then you went in?

Dimitri

I went in.

Groushenka

Dimitri—There—on your sleeve—it's blood, isn't it?

Dimitri

Blood—human blood. And God! Why was it shed? (The chorus

of the daughters of Mokroie explodes outside. Dimitri stands up) Ah—the singers! (He runs to the terrace. They acclaim him.) Come up! Come up! (Dimitri greets the crowd on the terrace.) Hello! Well, yes, it's Dimitri Karamazov—once again, one more time! You recognize me?

Dimitri

I'm coming to see you. To have a party with you—there's champagne—hold on—(He passes out bottles) Cognac, Rum. I thought of you, Vassiliev. Hello, Gregori. Here are cigars—if you don't smoke them, eat them. (Laughter) And there'll be some punch. Trifon—heat up some punch! They're going to serve food in every room. Go eat. Here are the musicians. (Enter Jewish musicians bearing lutes, violins and zithers) Boris, come on in,, will you! (He shakes his hands) Hello, hello—Is there some money? Ah, ah—300 roubles for the musicians. (He shakes his pile of roubles)

Groushenka

(Low) Will you put your money in your pocket?

Dimitri

(Low) Yes, it's shameful. I'm ashamed, Grousha. But the joy of being here!

Groushenka

Amuse yourself, go ahead.

Dimitri

Tomorrow, I'll go, I'll know how to go. Unpack what remains. There are bonbons and sugar candy. Hey, musicians, are you asleep? (He sings the tune he wants them to play) You are going to dance, play the fool. (To two girls who come in) Hey, Anna Stepanida! Reveal yourselves, will you, my beauties, so we can see you! (To Groushenka) Aren't they pretty?

Groushenka

Kiss them, fool! Fools like you please me. (Dimitri seizes each girl in turn and kisses her. The violins play. They do a dance step. The flame of the punch illuminates the court. All shout "The punch! Here's the punch!" And they rush to the stairs)

Dimitri

(Mixing with the crowd that accompanies him) Go drink! And gaiety, uproar. I want everybody to be shitfaced by dawn. I intend for it to go on until noon tomorrow. (He goes back into the room staggering a bit, and stops in the door way) Until tomorrow noon—and all will be over with.

Groushenka

Mitia come back. You are forgetting me. I see that you are sad. Why? Oh, Mitia, Mitia—to say that I loved him so much for five years. Coming here, I asked myself how we'd look at each other, what would be our first word—And when I saw him—it seemed to me that a bucket of excrement fell on my head. I won't speak of it again, Mitia, don't go way, my pigeon, I have something to tell you. Listen: I love someone here—Tell me who it is.

Dimitri

(Struggling against his happiness) No.

Groushenka

Someone came in here just now and joy followed him! And my heart said: "Stupid. There's the one you love!" Mitia, think only about me. Mitia I love someone here. Do you know who it is? I am going to tell him.

Dimitri

(Covering his ears) No, no, don't say it. I couldn't take any more. All I've done doesn't count, whatever I did was good so long as I thought I'd lost you. Do you understand? When I came in here—after this race—Oh, the fresh air on my face. The night full of stars, yes, joy was following me. Meaning my soul was torn apart, but I was almost content, almost satisfied, yes—because it was all over—seeing you again, merely seeing you again, and then it was over—I was determined. I felt for you nothing but a tender love—a completely new love full of abnegation. No—no jealously, no hate against that man. He was your first lover. You waited for him, loved him, for five years. I thought that you still loved him. I thought you were happy, Grousha. I no longer needed life. Life for me, no longer had any feeling, no value. Ah, I was advancing toward death. And now, now here when you are opening your arms to me—.

Groushenka

(pulling him) Mitia, I love you! Will you forgive me for your sufferings, my Mitia? Love me! I am no longer the same today, I've understood. No one has loved me the way you loved me.

Dimitri

But the blood!

Groushenka

Kiss me, don't listen to me. He kisses me, and then he looks at me and listens to me. Why do you listen to me? Kiss me! Harder! Harder! That's it. When one loves!

Dimitri

So much the worse!

Groushenka

Yes—so much the worse!

Dimitri

For this minute I would have given my life. I no longer wish to think of anything. I haven't any thoughts. Grousha—I am happy!

Groushenka

Let's drink! (She fills the glasses)

Dimitri

Ah, may my heart be strong enough to contain its joy! May the night last long enough so that the dawn may at last quench this thirst for joy.

Groushenka

(Lying back in an armchair she presents her glass to him) Mitia, I am drunk and you are not.

Dimitri

I am drunk from something other than wine!

Groushenka

They are still dancing below.

Dimitri

Come see them.

Groushenka

I want to dance, too. (They are before the open window) Ah—night—heaven is getting pale already. (She staggers. Dimitri supports her in his arms) Carry me away, yes—(Dimitri places her on the bed; his kisses are more urgent) No, no—don't touch me, not yet. Spare me, Mitia, I beg you. My Mitia, yes, I am yours, but not here beside these people.

Dimitri

(On his knees) I obey. Not even the thought.

Groushenka

I know. You are a wild animal but your heart is noble, your heart is gentle. Do you see, it's our last folly—this night. Henceforth this must be proper, proper forever. Not your mistress, your wife. Alyosha said words to me today that I won't forget in my life. Stay this way. Don't budge! (Her voice goes weak) I am your wife. You will take me far away. A sledge is waiting for us; Mitia. Ah, now that we are leaving—how fast it goes. It's all white. There's snow. I love snow so much. One can hear almost nothing. It seems that one is no longer safe on earth. I'm fine, I'm tired Mitia—Mitienka. (She falls asleep. Dimitri watches her sleep for a moment, then rises. His glance wanders about the room. The candles are consuming themselves. He goes to the window. The songs are dead. A great silence reigns. Day comes. Dimitri shivers; little by little he gets hold of himself. Again he goes to Groushenka and looks at her. Finally he puts the gun to his head. Groushenka wakes up.)

Groushenka

Mitia, I'm cold. Where are you? What are you doing? (She leaps out of the bed and goes to him)

Dimitri

It's dawn. I can no longer live. I've sworn it.

Groushenka

(Snatching the pistol from him) Why do you want to die? You are afraid?

Dimitri

I'm not afraid. I'm shamed, shamed.

Groushenka

Because of the blood?

Dimitri

The blood is nothing—but the money.

Groushenka

What money?

Dimitri

Katherina's money that a week ago I placed against my breast. I threw it to those girls, those musicians. I am a thief.

Groushenka

We will return her money. I will give you what is necessary. All that is mine is yours now! We will go ask pardon of the Miss and then we will leave. Give her back her money but love only me! If you love her, I will butcher her.—I will scratch her eyes out.

Dimitri

I love only you! I will love you in Siberia.

Groushenka

We will work. We will do penitence. God will pardon us. I still know how to pray to God. Alyosha said it is necessary to work. I will work for you. I will be faithful to you. I will be your slave.

Dimitri

Yes. One can live in Siberia. Down there one can love and suffer. I'm not afraid. There, my beloved, under the ground in the depth of ruins, in suffering—we will sing a hymn to the God of joy.

Groushenka

Ah! Mitia—we are going to live. If bad, so be it, it's so good to live!

Dimitri

Near you! (Presses her against his heart) (Silence)

Groushenka

(Startled, in a strangled voice) Who's looking at us there? (Dimitri follows her look and sees a man standing in the door way. He leaps toward him)

Chief of Police

(In a deep and firm voice) Come with us, if you please. (Dimitri takes a step. Behind the door are visible a crowd of Mouzhiks and soldiers)

Dimitri

(Shouting) Ah—I understand (He weakens and faints in a chair)

Chief of Police

Lieutenant Karamazov. I have to inform you that you are accused of the murder of Feodor Pavlovitch Karamazov. Murdered last night.

Dimitri

Never! (Starting) I am not guilty! Not that blood, I am not guilty! I didn't shed my father's blood.

Groushenka

Thank God!

Dimitri

Yes, I wanted to kill him. But I didn't kill him. It wasn't me. It wasn't me!

Groushenka

He's telling the truth. Believe him. (On her knees before Dimitri clasping his knees) I believe you, I believe you. (At a gesture from the chief of police, soldiers fill the room)

CURTAIN

ACT V

Feodor Pavlovitch's. The salon. Same décor as the 3rd act, two months later. It's the beginning of winter in the afternoon. Gregory enters his head wrapped in a bandage.

Gregory

(Turning) Well, aren't you coming in? (Smerdiakov enters with barely perceptible hesitation. He holds a small package of clothes in his hand. His face is pale and ravaged. They cross the stage in silence. Gregory sits, head in his hands)

Smerdiakov

You are still suffering?

Gregory

It was a frightful blow. And you—how you've changed!

Smerdiakov

For the last two months, I've had one crisis after another. They thought at the hospital that I wouldn't pull through. (Silence) (Smerdiakov looks around him) It was here that they found him?

Gregory

There, stretched out in front of the icon.

Smerdiakov

Dead?

Gregory

Yes. (A silence) They say that since his condemnation Dimitri Feodorovitch's become a different man—that he weeps for his sins.

Smerdiakov

Twenty years in Siberia, that's tough.

Gregory

The unfortunate. I who washed him in his little bassinette when he was a child—he dared! Ah, when I noticed the master's window wide open, right away the presentiment grasped me. I was awakened abruptly, toward midnight, and remembering not having locked the key in the garden gate, I went out. At the same moment I saw a shadow, about four steps away, fleeing rapidly. I rushed at him to cut his escape and I reached the palisade exactly at the moment that Dimitri scaled it. Ah, I indeed recognized him. I grabbed him by the leg, shouting. But he unloaded such a furious blow on my head that I released him and rolled motionless on the ground. Some hours later they arrested him at Mokroie!

Smerdiakov

Who actually gave the alarm?

Gregory

My wife. Not seeing me come back, she emerged in her turn, she screamed; people came. That's when they discovered the cadaver of the Master. And the next morning they found you in the cellar, fainted, foam in your lips—in prey to a frightful epileptic crisis.

Smerdiakov

That's what they told me at the hospital. I don't remember anything; anything.

Gregory

What a misfortune, my God.

Smerdiakov

And Ivan?

Gregory

Ivan Feodorovitch didn't return from Moscow until two days after the burial. Since the trial he hasn't budged from here.

Smerdiakov

And what's he say?

Gregory

About what?

Smerdiakov

About Dimitri's conviction.

Gregory

Nothing. Always shut away, always somber. He cannot endure anyone. Alyosha comes rarely. He never leaves the prison. Only Katherina Ivanovna.

Smerdiakov

They see each other often?

Gregory

Very often.

Smerdiakov

Here—?

Gregory

Yes.

Smerdiakov

The somber tragedy might actually end in a marriage. (A silence) He never asked news of me?

Gregory

Who?

Smerdiakov

Ivan

Gregory

Never.

Smerdiakov

Maybe he thinks I'm dead. (Ivan enters. He says nothing. Gregory wants to address him but the closed face of Ivan curdles that desire. A long silence. One feels that Ivan cannot speak and Smerdiakov cannot leave.)

Smerdiakov

I left the hospital this morning.

Ivan

You are going to resume your service here?

Smerdiakov

It's my intention. (Gregory leaves by the right. Silence)

Ivan

You know then?

Smerdiakov

I believe that you are sick, too. Why are your eyes so yellow?

Ivan

Leave my health out of it and answer my question!

Smerdiakov

How could I not know? Everything was certain in advance.

Ivan

Even your crisis?

Smerdiakov

Ask for clarification about my illness from the doctors in the hospital. What do you want me to say to you?

Ivan

You precisely indicated the cellar.

Smerdiakov

Because I was afraid in that cellar where I was far from all help. I always said to myself, "It's going to come. Am I going to fall?". And it was effectively at this thought that the spasm seized me, and that I fell. I told that to the doctors and the investigating judge—they were of my opinion.

Ivan

Ah?

Smerdiakov

Why should I lie? Do I have something to fear?

Ivan

All that doesn't explain why you were so eager to see me leave for Tchermachnia.

Smerdiakov

I sensed the evil. The house wasn't secure. I wanted to distance you from it.

Ivan

You wanted to distance me from the crime?

Smerdiakov

You didn't guess it?

Ivan

I would have stayed.

Smerdiakov

I understood that you were afraid and that you knew.

Ivan

Do you think I'm as cowardly as you are?

Smerdiakov

Excuse me, I thought so.

Ivan

(After hesitating) Dimitri formally accused you before the court.

Smerdiakov

That's all he could say with the charges weighing on him. He was trying to save himself. You see he wasn't able to do it. (Ivan becomes silent, Smerdiakov goes to him and touches his arm) Look, Ivan Feodorovitch, if I had bad designs on your father, do you think I would have been stupid enough to go tell you all that I told you?

Ivan

I'm not accusing you. It would be ridiculous to accuse you.

Smerdiakov

I have confidence in you like in God. Can I go to my room?

Ivan

Go. (He watches Smerdiakov go upstairs then turns away to see Katherina Ivanovna in the door way. He rushes to her and takes her in his arms)

Katherina

(Pulling away a little) You are feverish. You are burning me.

Ivan

(Holding her again) Each day, I ask myself if you will come. You come, but to resist me.

Katherina

We must wait.

Ivan

What?

Katherina

Let me appease myself.

Ivan

I want you.

Katherina

Be more patient. Since I am in your arms. Since I am happy in your arms. (She lets her head fall on Ivan's shoulder and weeps)

Ivan

Oh! You are ill, right?

Katherina

Don't doubt my love, Ivan.

Ivan

I never knew you more joyful when you weren't giving in.

Katherina

I've only got my love, Ivan! You dispossessed me of all the rest.
(Groushenka appears in the door way)

Ivan

(Brutally) What's this?

Groushenka

(Taking a step) Alyosha isn't here? He ought to come after leaving the prison. I'm going to sit outside and wait for him. (Starts to leave)

Katherina

(Taking a step towards her) Madame. Do you sometimes see Dimitri in prison?

Groushenka

Every day.

Katherina

Does he already know—his brother and I—have decided to make him escape?

Groushenka

What? You intend—?

Ivan

It's necessary. Everything is prepared. I've got money. The

leader of the relay station has promised his help.

Groushenka

And Dimitri consents?

Ivan

Alyosha has taken charge of sounding him out.

Katherina

His reply?

Ivan

I'm waiting for it. (Groushenka makes a face to withdraw)

Katherina

Madame. You saw him this very day?

Groushenka

This morning.

Katherina

What's he doing?

Groushenka

He's talking. He's talking.

Katherina

What's he say?

Groushenka

Often things that I don't understand, but so beautiful that I cannot prevent myself from crying.

Katherina

Sad?

Groushenka

No. Gay, rather. But when he starts striding in his cell rummaging in his hair I see plainly that something is troubling him.

Katherina

Yes.

Groushenka

A secret. The imbecile. I know his secret. (Lowering his eyes) He doesn't love me. He thinks about you. He talks to me of you!

Katherina

(With a deep exaltation) Yes, I wounded his soul; he wounded mine—for all our lives.

Groushenka

He repeats that if you refuse to come, then he will still be unhappy. Do you hear? He dares to say that to me. (Very low) You must come.

Katherina

I cannot. He will look at me. No—

Groushenka

Don't you have pity?

Katherina

Groushenka, on my behalf—will you kiss his hand? Tell him that our love is dead but that he remains cruelly dear to me. Oh!—let him not stop loving me! Tell him. (Groushenka shakes her head but curtsies deeply) Tell him—and forgive me.

Groushenka

We are both bad, my little mother. You don't need my pardon nor I, yours. But save him, and I will venerate you all my life. (Alyosha enters)

Ivan

(To Alyosha) Well?

Alyosha

He refuses. The convoy of exiles departs in an hour for Siberia!

Ivan

Why does he refuse?

Alyosha

"They're offering me freedom without believing in my innocence. I don't want that." That's his reply. He told me also "I don't wish to steal my purification from myself." He's full of strength and joy.

Ivan

You're the one who prevented him from accepting.

Alyosha

No, brother. But God has visited him and he has a thirst for suffering. He wants to go to penal servitude for the salvation of all. Poor Mitia! Always bold. No doubt he's not yet prepared for such a martyrdom. In prison the familiarity of his guardians already revolts him. Down there, if someone strikes him he won't accept the affront. And that's when he will kill.

Ivan

You said—"That's when he will kill."

Alyosha

Yes.

Ivan

As if he had not killed already?

Groushenka

It wasn't him—

Alyosha

Dimitri didn't kill our father—No, Ivan.

Ivan

You have proof?

Alyosha

The word that he gave me. I cannot doubt him.

Groushenka

Dimitri is incapable of lying.

Ivan

Is that all you oppose to the sentence of the judges?

Alyosha

They could only condemn him. Everything overwhelms him. All that can be explained works against him. More than presumptions, almost proof.

Katherina

His hate against his father.

Alyosha

He wasn't the only one to hate him.

Ivan

He never stopped proclaiming his plan to kill him.

Alyosha

The facts howl. But, for feelings, that's another matter.

Ivan

The morning of the crime, he would have smashed him if I hadn't held him back. At eight in the evening he left Katherina like a fury, going to his father's.

Alyosha

Because he thought he'd meet Groushenka there. She wasn't there.

Ivan

Look, look—an hour later he came in here, searched the house, and lay in ambush behind the hedge. From that moment he was in ambush. That very night they found father murdered and in the garden, Gregory almost smashed. Dimitri admits he struck Gregory—and you deny that at the same hour in the same place, the same hand committed this double murder!

Alyosha

For which of us, Ivan, are you making this prosecution speech? I would have preferred to see you gather, in favor of our brother, the least presumption of innocence. Still, you've forgotten the accusation of theft which weighs on Dimitri, too. Is it because it appears to you less well founded? Feodor Pavlovitch kept 3,000 roubles hidden in an envelope about him. After the crime it was impossible to find either the envelope or the money.

Ivan

And the 3,000 roubles that Dimitri boasted of spending at Mokroie?

Alyosha

You know as well as I do where those 3,000 roubles came from. For several days he kept them against his breast wrapped in silk.

Katherina

I told the court they could represent the sum delivered by me into his hand and that it was correct.

Alyosha

Yes, you said it honestly as exculpatory evidence.

Groushenka

That's what Dimitri calls your betrayal!

Alyosha

Alas! My brother feels less loss of honor for murdering than for having committed this indelicacy. He considers it as the worst of his crimes.

Katherina

The most bitter of his humiliations.

Alyosha

Also, until the hearing he kept refusing to explain this point. After your revelation, didn't you see, Katherina, that he stopped defending himself and even that he accused himself?

Katherina

Yes, so as to have the last word, to leave me with remorse for having ruined him, to crush me with his superiority!

Groushenka

I saw you go pale at that moment. Ah the reply wasn't long coming. With what furor you screamed to the court that Dimitri, the evening of the crime declared to you "I'll return those 3,000 roubles to you, if I have to go to Siberia." If the least doubt remained in the minds of the jurors, that argument carried it off. It was over.

Alyosha

What. You are still fighting?

Groushenka

It's the young lady who did it all. She's the one who ruined him, she! You needed his conviction!

Ivan

So long as you won't bring evidence.

Alyosha

Let's no longer argue the evidence. What's the use? Dimitri

leaves in an hour for Siberia. How just the expiation may be for him, despite the injustice of the sentence—I admit it. Alone he must master his misfortune. He was capable of killing. But at the supreme moment God saw him. God touched that childish soul. He fled. It wasn't him!

Ivan

In that case, who? (Going to Alyosha, very low) Who, according to you is the murdered?

Alyosha

(Gently) You know quite well yourself.

Ivan

What?

Alyosha

You indeed know who—

Ivan

I'm waiting for you to say it.

Alyosha

It wasn't you. That's all that I can say.

Ivan

(Pulling him by the sleeve) Come on, come on. Explain.

Alyosha

Ivan, you've more than once said that you were the murderer.

Ivan

(A bit distracted) Why, when was that? I was in Moscow. I never spoke of it.

Alyosha

You said it many times when you were alone during these two terrible months. You accused yourself and you admit it. But you are not the murderer—you hear? It wasn't you. God has inspired me to tell you this even though you must hate me forever.

Ivan

Alexei Feodorovitch I have no taste for clairvoyants nor for divine messengers—you know that! From this moment I am breaking with your forever—and I beg you to leave me immediately.

Alyosha

My brother. If something happens today remember me, above all! Dimitri said to me this morning—"Ivan is superior to us, it's up to him to live!" Remember that, too.

Ivan

You are leaving? Where are you going, Lyosha?

Alyosha

Down there. In the mines. I will accompany Dimitri step by step. His ills are those that can be shared. And if he cannot endure his pain to the end he will need someone near him— who can answer for him. Let's go—(Groushenka who was seated rises and joins him happily)

Katherina

And Groushenka?

Alyosha

(Taking Groushenka's hand) Groushenka will be on the voyage, too. She accepts her cross. We will be doomed together.

Katherina

Not Groushenka!

Alyosha

(Taking Groushenka's hand) Goodbye. (He leaves holding Groushenka's hand)

Katherina

(Rushing after them) No!

Ivan

(Shouting) Katherina! (Katherina stops, upright against the door, twists her hands and watches Alyosha and Groushenka leave by way of the garden)

Ivan

(Close to Katherina, over her shoulder) Would you like to follow them?

Katherina

(Turning and throwing her arm over Ivan's neck) You see plainly I am obeying you. (Raising her hand) But didn't you hear what they just said? I'm the one who betrayed him, I'm the one who ruined him. I betrayed myself.

Ivan

(Discouraged) You still belong to that murderer!

Katherina

The way you speak of him.

Ivan

(With sudden violence, distracted) You too, you don't believe he's a murderer? You don't believe he's a murderer. You listen to what the others are saying. When I speak to you, you say to yourself "Who?" You walk in the street and you dream—and you think "This cannot be a dream." You sleep and you see. You wake up and you listen to a voice which tells you "Who, who really, who is this?" I said it all just now. You were there? I said, "Who, actually?"

Katherina

What's wrong with you, Ivan?

Ivan

In that case, in that case—if it's not Dimitri who killed—
(Becomes silent)

Katherina

What are you thinking about?

Ivan

I'm thinking of nothing. I don't think. There's something in my head—that thinks. You don't know what it is? You don't know what men think about. Like intoxication with wine, like the lusts of love—one cannot stop thinking like that. The man who thinks—what doesn't he think about?

Katherina

You're delirious!

Ivan

(Making an effort to get control of himself) No, no. I'm not delirious. Stay with me. I know where I am. I see objects. I hear. Do you hear upstairs?—He's installing himself.

Katherina

Who's that?

Ivan

Smerdiakov. He came back this morning. We need to talk together. I'm going to say a word to him. Leave us, Katherina. One moment. Go in there. I'm fine. Go. I will call you. Go, go, go. I'll soon be done. (He pushes Katherina out) (Ivan goes up to Smerdiakov's room. The door is locked, he shakes it.)

Ivan

Open up, Smerdiakov—it's me.

Smerdiakov

(Voice from his room) What do you want now?

Ivan

(Raising his voice) Open up!

Smerdiakov

(Half opening his door) I'm ill, sir. Leave me at rest, I beg you.

Ivan

(Grabbing him) I won't leave you. You will speak! I will force you.

Smerdiakov

Why are you torturing me like this?

Ivan

I Intend to know why you wished my departure?

Smerdiakov

That question again! I thought it resolved, by an intelligent man.

Ivan

I won't allow you to play with me. What cowardly understanding did you permit yourself just now? Yes, when I said it was ridiculous to accuse you, why did you reply, "I have confidence in you like in God?"

Smerdiakov

You actually desire that we speak with an open heart. An explanation?

Ivan

Am I in cahoots with you to fear it?

Smerdiakov

You have no more to fear from me than I from you. If you succeed in accusing me and what I reveal in my turn—the conversation that we had here—an hour before the crime—everyone would suspect your evil feelings and perhaps—another thing.

Ivan

What's this "other thing" again? Talk, stinking animal!

Smerdiakov

Why—why—if by chance you had desired the death of your father—(Ivan hits Smerdiakov on the shoulder with all his strength . Smerdiakov staggers and shivers) It's shameful of you, sir, to beat a weak man. (He weeps in his mustache)

Ivan

Enough! Enough, will you! Don't push me to extremes. You thought me in agreement with Dimitri about this thing?

Smerdiakov

I didn't know your feelings. It was to know them that I stopped you on the stairway.

Ivan

What? To know what?

Smerdiakov

Precisely if you wanted your father to be killed?

Ivan

By Dimitri.

Smerdiakov

Naturally. Dimitri, the murderer would lose all his rights. Half his share of the inheritance would go to you, giving you 60,000 roubles. I don't speak of your other desires.

Ivan

Listen, wretch. If I was counting on someone it was on you that I counted and not on Dimitri. It was possible to foresee some filthiness on your part.

Smerdiakov

You see plainly—you see plainly—And despite this presentiment you left.

Ivan

I had no presentiment. No, I swear I didn't.

Smerdiakov

No? You weren't expecting anything from me?

Ivan

Nothing.

Smerdiakov

Really? You refused to go to Tchermachnia despite your father's supplications. And, suddenly, on my advice, after all that I said to you, you announce your departure for Moscow!

Ivan

I never thought the thing was possible.

Smerdiakov

But you had that thought, you had it. Wouldn't a good son have delivered me to the police and have me whipped for my words—Why, no—you heard me complacently, you were really nice about all I said. What could I conclude?

Ivan

Enough! I don't fear you—I never had that thought.

Smerdiakov

(Going to him) Who cares—since you were running no risk. I tell you there's no evidence. See how your hands shake. Why? Go sleep in peace. You are not the murderer.

Ivan

They told me that already. I know it perfectly well.

Smerdiakov

(Accenting the words) You know it!

Ivan

Speak then, serpent! Say everything.

Smerdiakov

You haven't understood yet? Come on, we are here by ourselves. Why play a comedy to each other?

Ivan

Comedy? What comedy? I am not playing a comedy. (Looking at him with distraction) Ghost!

Smerdiakov

You are ill. There's no ghost here. There's only you, me and yet another person between us.

Ivan

Who? Who else?

Smerdiakov

God. God is here, near us.

Ivan

You lie! You're the one that's playing a comedy. You don't cease to lie to embroil me—to distract me—One cannot understand a thing that you say. Either you are mad or you are amusing yourself to exasperate me. Yes, you are mad, you are mad. I don't want to listen to you. Get out of here. You are mad. (He recoils in such a rush that he bumps his back—against the wall and stays there, nailed to the spot. He looks at Smerdiakov with terror)

Smerdiakov

(Looking at Ivan with mad hate) Wait a little. (He pulls his pants above his left knee, revealing a white sock, a buckle and garter and plunges his hand into his sock)

Ivan

(Stammering) Mad man! Mad man! (Smerdiakov pulls from his sock a packet of roubles which he places on the table)

Smerdiakov

There they are!

Ivan

What's that?

Smerdiakov

Deign to look. (Ivan goes to the table picks up the roubles which fall from his fingers) Are you going to faint? They're all there. Three thousand roubles. You don't need to count them.

Ivan

(Sits down with a sort of smile) You scare me.

Smerdiakov

Then truly, you didn't know?

Ivan

(After a silence, eyes lost, tonelessly) You were alone or with my brother?

Smerdiakov

I killed only with you, Ivan Feodorovitch. Dimitri is completely innocent. It's you who inspired me with the crime. I only accomplished it.

Ivan

(Crashed) Then I had the thought—I must have had it. God! For a thought!

Smerdiakov

It's necessary to hide this. (He hides the roubles under a book) You who have so much courage? (angrily) Don't tremble like that.

Ivan

(Almost submissive) Sit down and tell me everything.

Smerdiakov

How the thing happened? Why in the most natural way. You had gone. I hid myself. I waited. I was sure Dimitri would come over the fence at midnight to find out for himself what was going on here.

Ivan

(Raising his head) And he didn't come?

Smerdiakov

If he had nothing would have happened.

Ivan

God! God! Speak without hurrying. Don't forget any detail.

Smerdiakov

He couldn't not come. I had prepared him so well, for the last three days.

Ivan

Stop! Why did you kill?

Smerdiakov

The words that you uttered—

Ivan

Never mind my words! But the motive, the interest that drove you?

Smerdiakov

From disgust, from vengeance—and also for the money.

Ivan

But if Dimitri had killed he would have taken the money.

Smerdiakov

He wouldn't have found it. I told him the money was hidden under the mattress. It was behind the icon. The thing done—I seized the sum—and the whole thing passed onto Dimitri's account.

Ivan

Continue.

Smerdiakov

Continue? (Slowly) So be it! I waited then, in silence. In the night your father, called me, got restless. I didn't budge.

Suddenly.—The signal. I came out of my hiding place. Feodor Pavlovitch opened the window, leaned out calling. The window is low "He's going to strike him outside", I thought—But nothing. Time went by. My heart beat, I was going to run out of patience when your father, thinking no question that Groushenka was waiting for him at the small door took the lamp and went out. He stayed outside maybe one, maybe two minutes. Blood rushed to my head, my breath failed me. Finally, coming from the depth of the garden, I heard a great scream. It was Gregory's voice. Immediately I understood that Dimitri seized by fear, had fled, that Gregory on watch had caught him and a great struggle was taking place between them. If I didn't have the courage, the strength to profit from the circumstances and to accomplish the work myself, it was all going to start over. At the scream uttered by Gregory, Feodor Pavlovitch, shocked, came back in hurriedly. As for me, I was hidden behind the pillar. The old man hadn't taken three steps, when rushing him, I seized the cast-iron paper weight—here—this is it—it weighs three pounds and I struck him on the head with all my strength. He came in by the corner. He didn't even let out a cry and fainted. I struck him a second, a third time. I noticed then that his skull was cracked. He fell over, all covered with blood. I wiped off the paper weight—put it back in its place, I took the money from behind the icon and went out trembling. In the garden I went to the apple tree with a cavity—you remember? I'd noticed it a long while ago. I'd even prepared a dish cloth and a paper. I wrapped the 3,000 roubles in the dish cloth, the dish cloth in paper and hid the package in the back. It remained there for two months. I took it out this morning when I returned. Then, I ran to the fence and found Gregory there, lifeless, still breathing, and perhaps able to witness Dimitri's passage and accuse him at the same time, consequently of the crime and the theft. I was reassured.

Ivan

And then?

Smerdiakov

(Smiling) Then—I had my crisis.

Ivan

A real crisis or one you actually feigned?

Smerdiakov

Evidently, I was feigning. And the next morning I had a real crisis, the strongest that I've had in many years. I was unconscious for two days.

Ivan

Fine, fine—and then?

Smerdiakov

It's over.

Ivan

I don't see in all this why you needed my consent?

Smerdiakov

If by chance suspicion had fallen on me, you would have defended me.

Ivan

(Between his teeth) You wanted to torture me for my whole life! And thus assure yourself of impunity. But this impunity, you had it—in that case—why did you make me this confession? I'm going to denounce you! You can shut up, you could deny it.

Smerdiakov

My hate is stronger, Ivan Feodorovitch—I couldn't resist, it's the need for vengeance. I've hated you for so long. You never understood my worth—because I was a lackey. You insulted me, me who admired you so much—who forced myself to be valuable to you, who imitated you in everything. I was unable to endure that you would escape. I hate all Russia, sir—but it's you especially that I hate.

Ivan

(Picking up the book that covers the roubles) You showed me this money to convince me?

Smerdiakov

(In a trembling voice) That money, take it. I no longer have need of it. I thought that with that money. I'd begin a new life in Moscow. You were always talking about a new life. Or better still abroad, after I'd completed my instruction. Me, too, I thought to see those happy lands of Europe. It was my idea. I told myself that everything was permitted. (Raising his eyes to Ivan) You taught me that, because you taught me many things. If God does not exist there is no virtue—because it would be useless. That seemed true to me.

Ivan

And now what do you think—since you are giving up the money?

Smerdiakov

No. I don't believe it. (Strangled voice with a gesture of despair) Why then did you say that everything is permitted? And now, why are you so pale and your legs are shaking?

(With unspeakable scorn) You don't acknowledge even that; I did what you didn't dare to do. You don't dare even to kill me. You don't dare a thing—you, who used to be so audacious! You are going, perhaps, to ruin me, to accuse me in a cowardly way? (With anguish) No, you won't do that, Ivan Feodorovitch. That cannot be done. You are too intelligent, too proud. You love women, independence, luxury. You don't want to spoil your life. Of all the children of Feodor Pavlovitch you are the one who resembles him most. It's the same soul. (Ivan lets out a roar in terror) Come on, my former master, take the money!

Ivan

What money? Ah—yes—(He seizes the roubles and jams it in his pocket)

Smerdiakov

Hold on. Show it to me one more time. (Ivan pulls it out, Smerdiakov looks at it avidly without touching it)

Smerdiakov

Go, now—Ivan Feodorovitch! Goodbye. (He escapes and climbs

up the stairs running with effort)

Ivan

(As if still replying to Smerdiakov) Till tomorrow. Yes, I will go, for such is my will, not because of your threats and your challenge. Tomorrow, I will go to spit in their faces. All of them! Tomorrow only. Let's put everything off until tomorrow (Sneering) And from here until tomorrow. (Turning) What, you are sneering? Because you recognized your thought in my words? Anyway, you can remain. It's all the same to me. You don't exist. No, you don't exist. You—You're me. You are my illness, my hallucination—the incarnation of my thoughts and my most ugly feelings. You are merely me in another shape, the shape of a lackey! What—my mind was able to engender you? Sit back down right away. You horrify me! No—I shall resist! They shan't take me to the mad house. Get out! Get out, will you! (He seizes a glass from the table and hurls it at the vision. The glass breaks) Ah, ah, ah. (Calling) Katherina! Katherina!

Katherina

(Enters running) Ivan!

Ivan

Come, come—Oh—do you know how one becomes mad? Do you believe that one can observe oneself when one is in the process of going mad?

Katherina

Hapless Ivan.

Ivan

My love. (Pushing her away) I am a murderer—it was me!

Katherina

You are allowing yourself to be abused by a dream—

Ivan

No, no, no—it wasn't a dream. He was seated right there, on the divan. I threw a glass at his head—here are the pieces. He was certainly on the divan. (Laughing) It is terribly stupid.

Katherina

Who are you talking about?

Ivan

The devil! He haunts me. But he's lying. Ah, you see, the spirit doesn't know everything.

Katherina

Where is Smerdiakov?

Ivan

(Pointing to the paper weight) Three blows—with that! A thought, a single thought sufficed to put us in agreement. Katherina, darling, trust me, I'm not yet crazy! I'm telling the truth. (Giving her the 3,000 roubles) Here.

Katherina

What?

Ivan

The proof.

Katherina

Money proves nothing. Ivan, listen to me. Reflect. Smerdiakov is accusing himself from evil. He profited by the crime without having accomplished it. He prepared everything. Carefully . But he didn't have the courage. (On Ivan's face, as he listens avidly appears a last light of hope. He kisses her hand passionately murmuring, "Oh—Katherina". Then leaping to Smerdiakov's room. He pushes the door open violently, then recoils letting out a shocked scream)

Ivan

Hanged—there—I see him—hanged himself from a nail. (Katherina rushes to join Ivan who stops her with a gesture) No wait! (Ivan goes into the room. He soon reemerges, trembling in all his members—but his face shines with a sort of joy) It wasn't a vision. I touched his body. (A finger on his lips, he comes down the stairway stumbling) Hush! Katherina, don't call. He is dead. (Stops to laugh softly) Ah—ah—A riddance. May he take all the evil with him. I knew indeed it wasn't I—completely—

Katherina

Dimitri! Dimitri!

Ivan

Let him rot in prison! I don't wish to serve a God I do not believe in! I'm suffocating. (He staggers, Katherina supports him. Comes down stairs leaning on her)

Katherina

Come, come, lean on me.

Ivan

Katia, Katia—

Katherina

(Dragging him toward the divan) Here—lie down—

Ivan

(Hanging on her) Not death—not death—Katia.

Katherina

I am near you.

Ivan

Your scorn, so be it—Not death—I can no longer talk. I can no longer think. Even your hate, Katia, and all the tortures of the next world—so long as I still live. So long as I live. (Katherina holds him in her arms. She cradles him like a child)

CURTAIN

ABOUT THE AUTHOR

Frank J. Morlock has written and translated many plays since retiring from the legal profession in 1992. His translations have also appeared on Project Gutenberg, the Alexandre Dumas Père web page, Literature in the Age of Napoléon, Infinite Artistries.com, and Munsey's (formerly Blackmask). In 2006 he received an award from the North American Jules Verne Society for his translations of Verne's plays. He lives and works in México.

www.ingramcontent.com/pod-product-compliance
Lightning Source LLC
LaVergne TN
LVHW041619070426
835507LV00008B/331